LOVES
GOD
LIKES
GIRLS

LOVES
GOD
LIKES
GIRLS

A MEMOIR

SALLY GARY

LEAFWOOD
PUBLISHERS

LOVES GOD, LIKES GIRLS
A Memoir

L E A F W O O D
P U B L I S H E R S

Copyright 2013 by Sally Gary

ISBN 978-0-89112-359-0

Printed in the United States of America

Scripture quotations, unless otherwise noted, are from The Holy Bible, New International Version. Copyright 1984, International Bible Society. Used by permission of Zondervan Publishers.

Author's Note
As with any memoir, the recreation of these stories reflects my memory. While I've consulted past journal entries and talked with people involved, my parents in particular, to accurately retell these stories, ultimately they are a recreation from my memories and perceptions of the events. On at least one occasion I've combined conversations with various people from different periods of time in my life, but in such a way as to accurately preserve what I took away from those moments. And the names of people mentioned in the stories have been changed to protect their privacy.

Cover design by Steven Pisano
Interior text design by Sandy Armstrong

Leafwood Publishers
1626 Campus Court
Abilene, Texas 79601
1-877-816-4455 toll free

For current information about all Leafwood titles, visit our Web site:
www.leafwoodpublishers.com

13 14 15 16 17 18 / 7 6 5 4 3 2 1

To my parents
Who gave me the world

Acknowledgements

Ever since I was a little girl, I've wanted to be a writer. I still wouldn't call myself a writer, but I do love to tell stories. And thanks to a lot of people, I'm learning to do that now on paper.

Thank you Berta Simons, Marjorie Neely, Gin Owens, Opal Wright, Jane McKee, Debbie Williams, Robbie Jeter, JoElla Tritton, George Carter, David Williams, Forrest McCann and Dave Merrill for teaching me to write.

Thank you, Florence Rowe, for teaching me to love writing.

Thank you, Phil Dosa, for telling your boss about this woman you knew with a story.

Thank you, Leonard Allen, for listening to Phil and taking a chance on an inexperienced writer and a subject fraught with risk. Thanks for believing in the God-story in me. I have been blessed by your encouragement, your expertise in publishing, and your heart for people who are hurting and in need of a safe place.

Most of all, Leonard, thank you for connecting me with my editor, Lissa Halls Johnson. Lissa, without your help, this book wouldn't exist. Thank you for sifting through thousands of words, praying over all the stories, and pulling together precisely the right mix. Thank you for talking me through all my doubts and fears. My gratitude to you and Leonard for your personal attention to the crafting of this message goes far beyond this page. Thanks to all of you at Leafwood for caring deeply about this project.

To friends who have read snippets of the manuscript here and there, sometimes offering reassurance, sometimes saying, 'no, try again,' thank you. To preachers and professors who have spoken truth into my life over the years, from pulpits and over coffee cups, in your offices and in airports, thank you. For allowing me to question, to doubt, knowing all the time we were seeking God together. You have no idea how important those moments were to me.

To my personal village—to friends who walk beside me daily and to those who walk with me from a distance—thank you for holding me accountable, for loving me in the midst of all my messiness, for simply being with me and reminding me who I am. For feeding me, for cups of tea and pots of coffee, for listening to me go on and on and on, thank you, my sweet friends!

To my brothers and sisters who have shared their own journeys with me, thank you for trusting me with your stories. Your stories are a part of my story, no matter how different they may be, and they deserve to be told, too.

To David, for beginning this journey with me. For being just what I needed at the time. For countless hours of guidance, support and love, thank you. I won't ever forget.

To my mama and daddy, thank you for loving me fiercely. For believing in me more than anyone has ever believed in me. I am proud and most blessed to be your daughter.

And thanks to Chester, the world's greatest dog, who simply brings me joy.

Contents

I. The Lies Are Planted

II. The Lies Take Root

III. The Lies Grow Deeper

IV. The Lies Unearthed

V. Living in the Tension

I

The Lies Are Planted

Beginnings

When I was three years old my grandparents brought us a dog, a dachshund puppy that was only a few months old, with a plain rope looped around his neck for a leash. We named him Fritz, bought him a collar and a basket to sleep in on the porch, and he was a part of the family for the next ten years.

My grandpa said they bought him for us because I needed a dog. Because I needed something to love.

I'm glad Papa knew that.

One day when he and I were in a department store waiting on my mother and grandmother to finish their shopping, I was bothered by another little kid in the store staring at me. Later, on the way home in the car, I asked him about it and he said that boy was only doing that because he'd never seen a little girl as pretty as me.

I'm glad Papa said that.

When I was little he told my mother to let me do some things by myself, so I'd know that I could. Like when I'd go stay with them, he'd let me go into McWhorter's grocery store and buy something all by myself. All I had to do was sign his name on the ticket. That always made me feel so big and important.

I'm glad Papa let me do that.

He died before I finished the second grade. And yet in those moments my papa gave me glimpses of who I really was, who I could become, that have always stuck with me. If he believed I was lovable, capable, and pretty, maybe I could believe that, too.

And I can't help but wonder where I might be had my grandfather lived longer.

Our individual stories fascinate me because they give us a glimpse into how we came to be who we are. I've spent a lot of time analyzing the elements of my own story. But understanding it in my head doesn't necessarily fill the needs that are inside me. Sometimes I'm still that same little girl who needs to feel loved, to feel special, and to believe she can make it on her own.

And sometimes I can't help but wonder if our stories had been tweaked a little bit here and there, if more of our needs had been filled along the way that things might've turned out different. If we might have grown up with a little more accurate picture of who we really are, who we were really meant to be. If we'd had more encounters with someone like Aibileen from *The Help*, reminding us, "You is kind. You is smart. You is important." Over and over and over. Until it became a part of our DNA. Until we breathed it in and absorbed it so that it filled us clear down to our toes.

That's how we learn the truth of who we are, who God made us to be.

The truth God wants us to live out of now. You know . . . the truth that sets us free.

I Have Decided . . .

I can't remember a time when I didn't know who Jesus was.

My mother says I was seventeen days old the first time they took me to church. This was in the days before fancy baby carriers, so she laid me on a pillow in the pew.

My mother tells me I got into my first theological debate when I was in my three-year-olds Sunday school class. We were studying all the animals that Noah took on the ark and the teacher was explaining that bears ate fish. I told her no, they didn't, they ate soup. Hadn't she heard the story?

When my cousins and I played church, our mothers helped us fix communion with grape juice and crackers. That was our favorite part. It didn't bother me that I didn't get to play the preacher or say a prayer or lead a song, because I was a girl. And in our church, if you were a girl, you couldn't do those things. But oh how I loved singing "Trust and Obey" at the top of our lungs and sporting grape juice mustaches back in my cousins' bedroom.

It was even more special the Sunday morning our teachers served us communion in the four-year-olds class. First, they passed around the big sheets of cracker like the ones I had watched my mother take in church, pinching off a tiny piece, placing it to her lips, and brushing off the crumbs that dropped in her lap. Then my teachers passed the shiny silver trays filled with tiny cups of grape juice, and we each got to take one.

Nobody made a sound. Even at our young age we knew it was a solemn ceremony.

Although we got to experience that meal in Bible class, they taught us that we wouldn't take it again until we had come to a decision on our own that we believed Jesus was who he said he was, that we wanted to make him Lord of our lives, and were baptized. I didn't yet understand all that. But I understood that eating that cracker and drinking that juice was about Jesus—that I was doing something Jesus wanted me to do. And that was all that mattered. It mattered very deeply to me. Even at four.

The first time I took communion in church, I was eleven. However, the journey that led me to acknowledging that I wanted to be a follower of Christ and be baptized began quite a while before that. In most Churches of Christ in the 1960s there were racks of pamphlets in the foyer on lots of different topics—including ones to help people know how to become a Christian. When I was in the fifth grade I read one that scared me to death. The pamphlet told the story of a milkman who was a nice guy, but even though his wife and children went to church, he didn't see the need himself. He believed in God, but he didn't feel it was important to "put on his Lord in baptism," which, in the Church of Christ, meant that you had taken on the symbolic death, resurrection, and burial of Christ and would now follow him.

When "the trumpet sounds" terrible things start to happen all over the world—earthquakes and people disappearing from their homes and families, some going to heaven. The milkman has to answer for his life, and when he tries to explain that he lived a good life and believed in God, it wasn't enough. He ends up going to hell, being separated from his family, and living in torment forever and ever.

Let me say that I wasn't the kid who needed to read that. I was the kid who couldn't watch the TV soap opera *Dark Shadows* in broad daylight after school. I didn't read Nancy Drew mysteries and I didn't care for the scary stories that kids tell each other at slumber parties or around campfires. I was the kid whose imagination was so vivid that I didn't need to see something—I didn't even need graphic description—because what I was able to create in my head was almost always worse. The night I read the milkman pamphlet in bed I didn't sleep much, but that's not what motivated me to be baptized.

In the fifth grade, at the age of ten, my immature idea of "obeying the gospel" was driven by the same motive promoted in the pamphlet, namely fear of God's wrath, fear of eternal damnation. What nobody realized is that my fear of God was nothing in comparison to my fear of water, especially if it required me putting my head in it. And I knew that being baptized meant being fully immersed in the baptistery at the front of the auditorium. The thought of being dunked in the water and being the center of attention was more than I could deal with. So I kept putting it off. I even told my parents that if I was in an accident or something to take me by the church building on the way to the hospital and baptize me first, just in case.

In my fourth and fifth grade Sunday school classes, my teachers, Lorene Greer and LouEllen Foster, did such a beautiful job of teaching me stories from the Old Testament that I now know more about Ahab and Jezebel and Elijah than I ever cared to know. They went way beyond the duty of volunteer Sunday school teachers by planning Bible Bowls and parties and a full-blown Bible Times Market Place. I'm so thankful for those women and the picture of God they painted for me.

But in the sixth grade something changed. Blaine and Susie Armstrong showed me Jesus.

Blaine and Susie were a young couple at our church who became my Sunday school teachers. Blaine was baldheaded with brown eyes and a kind, but strong countenance. He was a good teacher, a good storyteller, and I loved listening to him. Susie was thin with long brown hair, pretty and sweet, and even though they were married, they liked each other. You could just tell. While Blaine taught, Susie sat at the front of the class to the side and smiled at us.

Week after week we went through the Gospels, and week after week I began hearing the way Jesus loved people. People who hadn't been loved by anyone else. People whom no one else paid attention to. Women. Children. People who had done things that were bad. He even loved those who didn't love him back.

When school was out for the summer, my mom made arrangements for me to go to Blaine and Susie's one afternoon to swim in the pool at their apartment. Because I was so afraid of water, I hadn't yet learned to swim, even though I wanted to. By that time I was too embarrassed to take beginner swimming lessons with a bunch of little kids. But I liked Blaine and Susie. I trusted them. And I felt completely safe with them in their pool, just the three of us.

I didn't learn to swim that day, but I think something more important happened. After receiving kind attention from a man who took a whole Saturday afternoon to play with a kid who wasn't even his, well, I listened even more closely to what he had to say in class after that.

By the middle of the summer our Sunday school class had worked our way to the end of the story of Jesus' life, and Blaine started telling us about Jesus' crucifixion. Telling us what it must have been like.

On that particular Sunday morning, instead of standing, Blaine sat on a metal folding chair, leaning toward us, clasping his hands in front of him. He went through every step Jesus took to the cross. He talked about all of his friends walking away while everybody else laughed and made fun of him. He told us how Jesus didn't fight back, how he didn't even try to explain or defend himself. He talked about the beatings and the long jagged spikes of the crown of thorns the soldiers pushed into Jesus' scalp. He explained how the robe must have stuck to the blood from the wounds on his back and when it dried, how painful it must have been when they ripped the cloth from his back and reopened those wounds. He told us how heavy the boards must have been when joined to make a cross—a cross strong enough to hold a grown man—so heavy that in Jesus' already weakened condition from no food, no sleep, and being beaten, he couldn't carry it alone.

I listened intently, in a way I never had, as though I hadn't heard the story all my life. But this time I didn't just hear it. For the first time I imagined what it must have been like. I felt the pain that Jesus must have felt.

By the time Blaine got to the part of the story where they placed Jesus on the cross, I thought my heart would break. Blaine stretched his hand out in front of us and showed us his palm. He took off his suit coat, sat back down and rolled up his sleeve a little, baring his wrist. He explained that the nails could've gone through Jesus' palms or his wrists to hold Jesus' body in place on the cross. And then he told us about the nails.

"Back in Jesus' day," Blaine said, "they didn't have access to a lot of metals, like iron or steel, to make nails or spikes as we know them today. So what they used instead were wooden pegs, carved sharply to a point at one end. But because wood isn't as sharp and strong as metal, it had to be pounded in harder to go through, and as it's pounded, splinters of the wood would break off."

As Blaine spoke, he pounded his fist into his palm, over and over.

I could already imagine how hard you would have to hit a wooden peg to drive it through your skin, but when I heard the word "splinter," I could totally relate. How many times had my papa dug splinters out of my fingers and hands with his pocket-knife? I knew what that felt like. I knew that splinters hurt, and that when they stayed in there and swelled up and got infected, it hurt even worse. Somehow in my eleven-year-old mind, that had no way of really grasping the depth of the physical pain Jesus must have endured, the thought of wooden spikes that split off into splinters into your hands and wrists was what put the whole experience over the top. My tender heart wanted to scream, "Stop! Stop! Don't do any more to him! He didn't do anything! Stop!"

It was at that moment that Jesus became everything to me.

All week long I thought about those wooden spikes going through Jesus' hands, and the more I thought about them, the more I realized I wanted to do whatever Jesus asked of me. And all my life, being baptized was one of the things I'd been taught that Jesus wanted me to do. After hearing everything Jesus went through for me, my fear of water became less of an obstacle to baptism.

In my church, baptisms occurred at the end of a worship service on a Sunday morning or evening or a Wednesday night. At the close of every service we sang what's called an invitation song and the preacher ended his sermon asking anyone who wanted prayer, to be baptized, or to place membership at that congregation to come down to the front, "while we stand and sing." Well, that's what most people did. But not me.

I didn't "go forward" or "respond to the invitation" at the end of that Wednesday night service. I had known for a long time that the moment I made that public declaration claiming Jesus as Lord, the minute I scooted in front of my daddy sitting at the end of the pew to walk out in the aisle and down to the front where the preacher was standing, that the tears would come. I was afraid to cry in front of all my friends, all those people sitting in the auditorium. It wasn't that I was ashamed of believing or ashamed of claiming Jesus. It was because I had been conditioned to believe that crying was a shameful thing, a mark of weakness.

So I waited until after we'd come home from church and were changing into our pajamas. I went into my parents' bedroom, sat down on the bed, and began talking to my mother about what I wanted to do. I don't remember anything about that conversation, except that there was never any talk of waiting until the following Sunday or even the next day. By that time it was around ten o'clock at night, but my mother got up and started calling people to meet us at the church building.

Our former preacher, the one I'd first known as a little girl, happened to be at our church that week for an evangelistic meeting. He was attending a get-together that evening with a lot of people from church. So when my mother called to ask him to baptize me, everyone who was at the party came as well. Just for me. Because they, too, knew it would be the most important decision I would ever make in my life—to follow Jesus. The very presence of these adults I looked up to reinforced what I already believed—that Jesus really was the most important part of our lives. That you drop everything and come to celebrate, support, and encourage; even if it's for an eleven-year-old girl who waited until everyone had gone home to make her desire known. Even when it was inconvenient to come back to the building, turn on the lights, and warm up the water. But they came. That meant the world to me.

I walked down the steps into the water, and Jimmy Jividen, the same man whom I had first known as preacher, took my hand and greeted me with his big expressive eyes and warm smile. He hugged me, took his handkerchief and dampened it. He softly explained that he would place that handkerchief over my mouth and nose as he lowered me under the water. He had no idea how afraid I was of the water and how out of control I would feel, especially being lowered backwards.

Everyone gathered around in the darkened auditorium lit with one spotlight. All I focused on was the man I had seen in the pulpit every week, long before I understood anything he was talking about. He was the man who had never walked past me without bending down and greeting me. The one who held the microphone for me while I said my memory verse at "pew packers" on Sunday nights. The man who showed me what preachers are supposed to be. So when he asked me if I believed that Jesus was the Son of God, there was no other answer but yes, oh yes, I believed.

God didn't remove my fear of going under the water that night, but he knew what a huge step of faith that was to a little girl terrified of water. And I believe that meant the world to him. The tears I shed coming up out of that water meant the world to him, too. For those tears reflected a heart touched by what Jesus had done for me. I was no longer motivated to be baptized and follow Jesus by fear, threat of punishment, or a parable of a milkman's fate. Love that endures pain and suffering moved me to follow Jesus and make that symbolic commitment to him.

I sobbed all the way back into the room where I dried off and changed my clothes. My mother was waiting to greet me, as well as the youth minister's wife whose voice I'll never forget. She kept saying, "Oh, sweet girl. Oh, sweet girl."

Back in the auditorium we circled up and held hands to sing the words that still touch me today: "I have decided to follow Jesus, no turning back, no turning back." They smiled at me as tears ran down my cheeks. They all hugged me and told me how proud they were of me.

Standing in that circle at age eleven, I didn't understand nearly all I've come to know, and all that I'm still learning, about what it would truly mean to follow Jesus. But I didn't have to. All that mattered was a tender little heart touched by the sacrifice of Jesus. A young girl who believed with all her heart that Jesus loved her.

. . . To Follow Jesus

To me, at age eleven, "following Jesus" meant that you went to church three times a week. You paid attention and participated in Bible class. You read your Bible at home and you talked to God. You went to Vacation Bible School in the summer and were involved in whatever was going on at church the rest of the year. Following Jesus meant that you were obedient to your parents and to your teachers, and you were nice to kids at school, especially the ones nobody else wanted to play with, even if the other kids made fun of you for it. Sometimes that was hard.

For me, it meant that I couldn't read *MAD Magazine* anymore, even though it was really funny, because some of it wasn't very nice. That was the biggest sacrifice I felt the need to make when I became a follower of Christ at the age of eleven. But it was sincere.

From then on I poured myself into soaking in everything, even when it seemed to others as though I wasn't taking anything seriously. I used humor to cover how deeply things touched me. And it seemed everything touched me. But at that age, I was uncomfortable letting anyone see how deeply I felt, certain that those deep emotions meant I was weak.

I went on my first mission trip to Aztec, New Mexico when I was thirteen, the summer before my freshman year of high school. We kids were sent out two-by-two on a door-knocking campaign to invite folks to the local church. I wasn't very happy that they paired me with a guy who was too bashful to initiate conversations with a stranger. He sat there, completely silent, while I did all the talking. Not that I expected anything different. The way I saw it, women do all the talking. All the teaching. Except from the pulpit.

I used the script I'd been given to begin asking these strangers probing questions and giving the right answers to theirs. My script had key passages I could use to teach them, hoping they would, at the very least, want to come to the services that week. Even better, that they would want more study or they would decide they wanted to become a Christian. I learned how to use the story of Phillip and the Ethiopian eunuch to show that baptism needed to be full immersion because, as the text says, they waited until they came upon a body of water large enough for them to "go down into the water" and "come up out of the water."

I became a leader in my youth group. I was the kid you could count on to be there, to participate in everything, and to answer questions in class when everybody else just sat there. I was the girl who didn't drink, though some of my friends in the youth group did. I was the girl who so sincerely believed that dancing was something you didn't do if you were a follower of Jesus that I had to tell every banquet and prom date that I wouldn't be dancing with them.

It helped that I was raised in a home where God came first in our lives—not only when we were at church, but every moment— even in the darkest moments, the moments I wasn't supposed to talk about. I was raised in a home where we talked about what God wanted for my life. Where I was taught Scripture and encouraged to rely on God for everything.

When I say I was "the good little Church of Christ girl," I truly was.

I say all of this, not to judge others or compare myself to anyone else, but to simply illustrate that my heart has always believed. I have always loved God and there's never been a time in my life when I walked away from him. Have there been times when I was angry at God? Yes. Times of questioning God—his purposes, his seeming passivity, his very existence? Yes. Yes. Yes. But walking away from God? Never.

Heritage

My father is one of the most tenderhearted, compassionate men I know. The kind of man who cries at anything involving a dog. Who befriends the kid at church with physical disabilities and invites him over to throw a football around in the backyard. Who decides to learn sign language so he can talk to a deaf kid nobody else talks to at church. Who believes he has a responsibility to give to others who are less fortunate, who haven't had the same opportunities as he had. The kind of man who gives to every charity that sends him something in the mail. Even when they misspell his name.

Where he learned all that I don't know.

Picture the Joad family from *The Grapes of Wrath* driving west out of the Oklahoma dust bowl of the 1930s to California, and that's as close to my dad's family as I can describe. A share-cropper for most of my dad's life, his father decided to move the family to California in the early 1940s during World War II where there were work opportunities in aircraft manufacturing. Prior to that time, my father attended a different school every year as the family moved from one rural community in West Texas to another in search of land my grandfather could work.

I think my father was the first person I learned to feel compassion towards. My mother told me stories about how he'd grown up as the youngest of three children, with a father who was emotionally disconnected from the family and a mother who favored his older brother—to the point of allowing him to abuse my dad. This cruelty went far beyond typical sibling rivalry. Being three years younger, Daddy was smaller, and his brother had the advantage over him physically. He held down my dad and smothered his face with a pillow or spat in his mouth until he cried, and then their mother whipped my father for crying. The boys' father, perhaps exhausted from tending fields as a sharecropper or working all day at the local cotton gin, sat most evenings in silence behind a newspaper, and hardly participated in family life beyond providing a living.

At the age of ten, Daddy overheard his mother tell a neighbor that she hadn't wanted him and that his birth had ruined her health.

During the Korean War both boys served in the military and Daddy's mother wrote letters to his older brother, sending my father the carbon copies.

When my parents got engaged, my father's parents invited them to come for dinner on a Sunday to celebrate. They lived about an hour's drive away, and my father explained to his family that he and my mother wouldn't be able to begin the drive until after church, so they wouldn't be able to arrive until early afternoon. That was all right, his mother told him. But when my parents arrived, not only had the meal already been eaten, but the dishes had been cleared and the leftovers put away. Because my father's older brother had to go to work that afternoon, they decided to go ahead and eat even though the whole meal had supposedly been planned in celebration of my parents' engagement.

Those incidents were some of many that perpetuated my father's lifelong belief that he wasn't wanted—a lifetime of feeling unloved. Of never feeling the security and sense of belonging in a family that God intended for each of us.

Even though he went to a different school every year, he excelled in his studies despite his family's lack of encouragement. They scoffed at him when he wanted to go to college, then later said that he probably should "since he couldn't do anything else." When he went on to obtain a master's degree, they thought it was a waste of time and money.

I've always marveled at my dad's accomplishments. Maybe that's why I've always liked movies like *Rocky* and *Rudy*, stories about guys who do big things without a lot of help from family. My dad was also without nurturing, encouragement, and support from parents and extended family, and yet he achieved what few people are able to even when they do have that support. I've been amazed at his determination—sure, sometimes motivated by anger, a sense of "I'll show you," coupled with a desire to be different from the family system that rejected him.

When I was a year old, my dad decided to give up smoking three packs of cigarettes a day, partly because of the rising cost of a carton of cigarettes and partly because he had accidentally burned me with one. He quit smoking that year by following a plan he read about in a *Reader's Digest* article and has never had another cigarette.

My mother's childhood was very different from his. Her parents were very much involved in the lives of their children. Her family was poor, living through the stock market crash and the resulting Great Depression. But my grandfather always had a job walking a pipeline for the oil company that later became Sinclair. My grandparents provided a home where my mother felt loved, nurtured, and encouraged to go to school. They weren't perfect, but they were good people. Neither of them had finished high school, but they sold furniture out of their home so they could send their daughter to college—something unheard of in rural communities in the late 1930s. And they were actively involved in church.

My father's family went to church sporadically, but it wasn't a guiding force in their lives. Sometimes he attended services with his friends or his cousins. When he joined the Navy during the Korean War, the man who became his closest friend was a Christian. But he'll tell you that it was my mother who taught him about Jesus.

My mom had been widowed for nine years when she met my dad. Her first marriage ended when her husband, Curtis, died of complications resulting from injury-induced diabetes. She had learned how to cook for him from the nutritionist at the hospital and became his eyes for him when the disease robbed him of his vision in the last year of his life. I grew up knowing as much about her life with Curtis as I did any other part of her history. I felt as if he was just another part of the family I would get the chance to meet in heaven someday. The first house Mama, Daddy, and I lived in was the same house Mama and Curtis lived in right before he died.

Being widowed at the age of twenty-nine in 1950 must've been hard for my mom. She got so lonely she'd drive to a shopping center and sit in her parked car and watch people go in and out of stores, just to feel less alone. Dusk, she said, was the hardest time. That's when she expected him to walk through the door from work, to eat dinner, and spend the evening together.

Couples from Mama's church made a special point of inviting her to do things with them and their families, and it made her feel good when they did. However, some women seemed jealous or nervous of her interaction with their husbands and children as though her singleness was a threat.

As a result of her experiences, my mother taught me a lot about how to be by myself, encouraging me to initiate contact with others. To be the person who reached out to people instead of waiting for them to include you. She talked about the parties she threw and dinners she prepared, about friends she made who helped her get through that time.

Between listening to how my mom made the most out of a painful time in her life, and watching *The Mary Tyler Moore Show* on TV, I grew up with a picture of single women different than most of my generation. I grew up thinking that, in contrast to the negative pictures of marriage that I saw, singleness might not be such a bad thing. In fact, it might even be better.

Mama began to date a guy named Will who worked for the same company, Mid-Continent Oil Supply, as my dad. One day, as she and Will were leaving for a lunch date, someone caught her eye. She nudged Will and asked, "Who's the cute new guy?"

She didn't date Will for very long after that.

When Mama was thirty-eight years old, a few years after she had first spotted the "cute new guy," she had her first date with my dad.

He invited her to dinner on a Wednesday night, and she told him that she went to church on Wednesday nights. He said he'd like to go with her, but that he didn't have a nice enough pair of pants to wear. They went to the nicest department store in town and bought him a pair of pants to go to Wednesday night prayer meeting.

I loved that story about a man willing to go to church with a girl on a first date. A man who cared about dressing appropriately because it was church—even if he was mainly interested in the girl.

One day, just six months later, the secretary of the elementary school where Mama was teaching first grade sneaked my dad into the storage room where they kept all the textbooks. My dad proposed to Mama there, giving her a beautiful engagement ring—a solitaire with a good-sized diamond set in a thin silver band.

They married on November 19, 1960 in the chapel at the church where I would grow up. Daddy's friends were an unseemly bunch who had threatened to kidnap him that night, all in good fun. But one of the older men from church sneaked my parents into his VW beetle and drove like a bat out of hell to lose the guys who were following them.

That story made the idea of getting married sound like fun. Like an adventure that you entered into with a boy you liked and who liked you, and you were in this together.

Papa

When I was a little kid I'd bring my toys into the den where I could be with everyone else. I'd drag my big sack of blocks that I kept in an old mesh grapefruit sack we brought home from the grocery store, clear down the hall from my room into the den and dump them out all over the floor. My mother said I could play with anything, anywhere, as long as I put it back where it came from.

I played with stuff that a kid could do by herself. I loved to read. I loved to play with Legos and Lincoln Logs. And with my Midge doll, Barbie's less attractive cousin. Midge came in a thin, black patent case where she lived with her clothes until Santa Claus brought Barbie's Dream House one year and she moved in with Barbie and Talking Ken.

I loved coloring books, and the smell of a new pack of Crayola crayons could almost make me drool. Sometimes when our wiener dog, Fritz, woke up from a nap he sauntered over and ate a few crayons left out of the box. He left colorful evidence that Daddy discovered when he mowed the yard, knowing which colors were missing before I did.

I loved to stay with my grandparents. Papa played Barrel of Monkeys and Pick Up Sticks with me until he got tired and had to rest. I'd keep playing on the floor in front of his recliner while he watched. He'd prop himself up with one hand on his knee and shift to one side in the chair, probably to help him breathe more easily. His lungs were racked with emphysema from working in the coal mines of southern Missouri as a boy and smoking a few too many cigarettes back in the day when real men rolled their own.

When he was having a hard time breathing, my grandmother might drive us around in the car where the cool air blowing in his face helped him to breathe more easily. I'd sit in between the two of them without a care in the world, perfectly content to be riding in the car, not really going anywhere.

Occasionally we'd drive to the lake outside the little town where they lived, and Papa let me hold a fishing pole in the water after he baited my hook. If we were riding anywhere after dark, we pretended the reflector lights on the side of the road were really a tiger's eyes.

I didn't like to eat eggs for breakfast, but every morning my grandmother fried me an egg so runny and half raw that it's a wonder none of us came down with salmonella. My Papa took a piece of buttered toast, fresh out of the oven so the butter was soaked into it, and pinched up little pieces in the egg. As he was fixing the bite he'd say, "Boy, I hope that catfish doesn't come up here and grab that bait off my hook. I've got to catch that catfish. He better not get that bait." Then he'd put that small bite of runny egg and toast all mixed together on my child-sized fork and leave it there on the side of my plate.

He'd look away or start talking to my grandmother standing at the stove behind us, fixing their breakfast. Then I was sup-posed to quickly gobble up the bite off the fork and put the fork back on the plate before he turned around to "check the line." Sure enough, every time the "bait" was gone. He'd act surprised and disgusted that he'd missed catching that pesky catfish again. I'd laugh and laugh until the bite of egg nearly fell out of my mouth. He'd fix another bite to "try again," and we'd repeat the routine until the plate was clean.

Papa loved to tell stories and I loved listening to them. Most of the time they were something completely farfetched, but he'd tell it as though it had really happened. And I believed him. Every word.

Like the story about the policeman who fell into the prickly pears and had to have the stickers removed from his rump! Or the giant grizzly bear who ate Papa's finger.

Papa's ring finger on his right hand had been cut off down to the last knuckle in an oil rig accident, but I didn't know that until I was an adult. Papa told me that a grizzly bear bit it off. And with all the bear hides covering the walls of his den—from bears he had shot himself—I surely believed him.

My favorites were the stories he created about places he and I were going to go and things we were going to do together. He talked about taking me on camping trips in the mountains where bears lived. And on our next trip, he'd say, we would surely find a little bear cub and bring it home to play with me. We planned and re-planned those trips to the finest detail, over and over. We'd talk about the people we'd take with us and what we'd fix to eat while we were camped out.

Sitting in the car with him so many afternoons, waiting on my mother and grandmother to finish shopping, we'd create these dream trips. I could see them all in my head so clearly. I think a part of me knew we weren't really going to take those trips. But it was so much fun planning and dreaming. It calmed me, soothed me, and gave me something to look forward to.

On days that he felt good, he took me out in the backyard adjacent to an open field and taught me how to shoot a BB gun. During our fresh-air drives, he had my grandmother drive us down country roads and when he spotted something to shoot at, he'd have her stop the car. Then as quietly as I could, I rolled down the backseat window, pointed the barrel of the gun out the window, and shot at whatever he'd seen.

In the days before portable oxygen tanks, Papa needed to go to the emergency room for his oxygen. It was a tiny hospital in a town with fewer than 10,000 people, and everyone knew my grandparents. After the nurse hooked up the oxygen and placed the mask on my grandfather, she let me sit with him. Just the two of us in this small emergency room furnished with everything you saw on those TV doctor shows like valves and tubes coming out of the walls.

They left the lights off, but the sun streamed in through the window enough for us to see each other. Papa sat in a wheelchair and made faces at me through the mask. I never felt the least bit afraid in that room, even with the tray of chrome scalpels and scissors and probes of every size imaginable laid out on a tray by the gurney. I think I've never been afraid of hospitals because of those hours I spent there with my sweet Papa when I was little.

When he came home from the hospital, he still didn't feel good. He'd lie down on the daybed in their living room and I stood beside him, combing the four or five hairs that still grew on top of his bald head.

The day Mama told me Papa had died I was staying at my friend Jennifer's house. That was toward the end of March in 1969, when I was seven. Mama and Daddy drove straight from the hospital to pick me up, and when I climbed into the front seat of our blue 1967 Chevy Caprice to sit between them, Mama pulled me close and explained that Papa couldn't get well, but that he was with God in heaven. "We'll see him again someday, Sally," she told me, "but we'll miss him right now."

I knew she meant that he was gone and that there would be no more Barrel of Monkeys, no more Catfish, no more shooting at blackbirds in the backyard, no more planning imaginary trips.

There would be no more Papa to talk to. And so I cried.

I still remember what his head felt like.

What my hand felt like, wrapped in his.

Mothers and Daughters

My first memories are of my mother, which are the safest, sweetest memories of much of my life.

Sitting on the floor with a coloring book and crayons, looking up at her, asking which color to use for people's skin in the picture.

Leaning up against her in the church pew, with her "tickle scratching" my arm that I stretched out across her lap.

Playing with homemade flash cards of colors, letters, and numbers, and with little plastic farm animals in church, all of which she kept in an old black coin purse.

Sitting next to her on the piano bench at home listening to her play by ear songs from the twenties like "Baby Face" and "Shine on Harvest Moon."

Lying on the couch with my head in her lap, watching TV in the evenings.

Even after I was an adult.

Even the mundane events of life with my mother left lasting impressions.

One of my earliest memories is of Mama washing my hair in the bathtub, holding me under the spigot to rinse my hair. I felt completely out of control, even though she was holding me. I was terrified of the water hitting me in the face. I was told you could hear my screams for someone to come rescue me from the impending doom of the bathtub faucet all the way down the hall. "Mammy, Papa, Santa Claus, Jesus, somebody save me!"

Before I started to attend school, it was usually just the two of us throughout most of the day. Every afternoon Mama put a quilt on the floor in front of the TV—which she left on—and that's where we'd nap together. Well, I'd lie there and watch TV while she slept.

In the springtime, my mother planted flowers in the backyard and in containers on our patio. She put birdseed in the feeders and made sure the birdbath was full of fresh, clean water. At dusk every night I stood with her as she went around the perimeter of the yard and watered the plants with the garden hose, holding her thumb just so and jiggling the hose so that it formed a shower on the leaves and petals, like a soft rain. We stood in the quiet and didn't talk at all. There might have been a show on TV I would have liked to watch or a book I wanted to read, but I preferred being with my mother. There was nowhere I felt safer than being with her.

My mother is the one who taught me right from wrong in almost every area of my life. She's the one who talked to me about God, about Jesus, about church. Mama taught me about life and people and relationships, and while everything she taught me might not have been exactly right, most of what she taught me was very wise.

I believed my mother was magic. Especially behind the wheel of a car. Whenever we were pulling up to a traffic light that was red, she began saying, "Change, light, change." And most of the time, miraculously, the light turned green and we kept right on going. Little did I know that she wasn't actually magical, but nonetheless gifted in her accuracy when it came to judging how much she had to slow down so she wouldn't have to stop. At those rare instances when she couldn't time it just right and ended up having to stop, she said the light was retarded. That was in the days before that word became something you didn't say.

My mother's driving reflexes were amazing. She had a lead foot so we didn't go anywhere slowly. Cars didn't come equipped with seat belts back then, and no one had ever heard of a car seat for a kid. In my case it didn't matter because my mother quickly extended her arm to hold me in place if she had to make a quick stop. She wasn't afraid to use the horn if the situation warranted it and didn't hesitate to shout things at the other drivers. At the very least, a driver who displeased her got one of her pointed looks as we drove past.

She told me stories about her life, about my family, about what it was like for her growing up. Sometimes I felt like I knew more about her era than I knew about my own. She told me about having been married before and what it was like to be a widow at the age of twenty-nine. She told me that she thought she would never have a baby of her own, and then she married Daddy and had me. She told me what a gift from God I was to her. And she told me over and over how she loved me more than anything or anyone in the world.

I never had a doubt that my mother wanted me and that she loved me dearly. As a result, I felt a great deal of responsibility to her—beyond simple obedience. I believed I needed to be perfect for her because she had already experienced so much pain in her life.

I never wanted to fall out of favor with her, and I couldn't stand it when she was upset with me. If I didn't do something she wanted me to, she stopped talking to me as much. Her whole countenance changed as she responded to me. When I reached adolescence, there were moments when I got furious with her, sounded off quite disrespectfully, and then stormed off to my room. But it wouldn't be thirty minutes before I couldn't endure it anymore. I couldn't bear being separated from her, so it didn't matter why I was upset with her, it didn't matter whether I was right or wrong, I apologized, always through tears. Nothing was the same with her until I apologized.

Fathers and Daughters

One of my earliest memories of my daddy, perhaps my first, is at church. They say that when we're little, before we acquire the gift of language, our memories are like snapshots. As we acquire the ability to use language to express ourselves, our memories become more like videos, like a motion picture with sights and sounds, smells even, making our memories more life-like. This memory is so early that it remains in still photographs pieced together, moving slowly and jerking, like something from the era of silent films, only in color.

In the Church of Christ, like other churches, we offer an opportunity for people who want to ask for prayers to come forward at the end of the service. People walked down the aisle from their seats to the front pew where the preacher was standing, holding his Bible, singing a cappella with the rest of the congregation. The song chosen for that time was usually something with lyrics that would hopefully touch people's hearts.

That particular Sunday my daddy stepped into the aisle and went to sit on the front pew where the preacher met him to take his request. He asked the preacher for prayer for him to be a better husband, a better father.

After the closing prayer, a mob of people moved toward the front to surround my daddy. Mama and I joined the flow moving toward him. He turned to face me for the first time since he left our pew, tears streaming down his face, sobbing.

So many people surrounded him that I couldn't get to him. I started crying, too. I couldn't stand seeing my daddy cry. At that moment, nothing else mattered. Our tears washed everything away, and all I cared about was wanting to be close to comfort my daddy. And I couldn't get to him.

I sat on the sofa next to Daddy, the open *Mother Goose* book in his hands.

"Daaaw-ktuh Faaaw-stuh," Daddy read in a very proper, upper-crust British accent, "went to Glaaa-stuh, in a puddle of raaaain."

I giggled. "More, Daddy!"

And so he'd read another *Mother Goose* rhyme in a different, yet just as silly, accent. "Jack Sprat, could eat no fat, his wife could eat no lean."

Mama said he was embarrassed, a grown man reading nursery rhymes, so he covered up by using funny voices. I didn't care why he did it, I just loved that he did.

Daddy had a knack for remembering limericks, funny songs, and jokes like nobody I've ever seen. Some of them weren't very nice, and my mother always stopped him before he got to the part that was a little risqué, but my cousins and I always got tickled when he started them, knowing what was coming.

"There once was a man from Calcutta—" he'd start out.

"Dan!" my mother interrupted. "Don't tell them that, you know that's not nice!"

He'd grin mischievously and roll his eyes, and we'd all laugh.

I hated going to the grocery store when I was a kid. The only enjoyment I found was rearranging the cans on the shelves. The manager of the store told my mother they loved it when I came to the store because the shelves looked so much nicer after we left.

Going to the grocery store with my dad, however, was a different story. Those times were rare, but on occasion, he'd go pick up something for my mom at the store, and I got to tag along. Standing in the check-out line, my dad always let me do something my mother would never allow. He let me buy Chiclets gum. They came in a yellow package where you could see all the tiny, miniature brightly colored pieces of gum through the oval cellophane window.

What I really liked about Chiclets—and what my mother didn't—is that you could pour them all into your mouth at once. Daddy let me chew the whole package in the car on the way home.

If Daddy went to the store by himself, he brought us surprises—usually candy bars. A Hershey bar with almonds for my mother, and Almond Joys for him and me. He's always called them "Al—mond" Joy instead of "All—mond" Joy, arguing that a man's name "Al" is pronounced with a short "a" vowel sound, so why shouldn't "almond"? If it's spelled the same, shouldn't it be pronounced the same? So I pronounced it that way. Just because he did.

Daddy also brought me special presents when he went on trips. Once he brought me a snow globe from Philadelphia. The best present, however, was from California. He brought back a *Batman* helmet and a blue cape, just like the one Adam West wore on the Batman TV show. Daddy and I liked to watch the show before it was time to go to church on Wednesday nights. We'd sit in the den after supper and watch Batman and Robin until my mother yelled from the back bedroom, "Dan! Are you ready for church?" He'd look at me and say, "Well, Sal? Let's go get ready."

Daddy built me a tree house in our backyard. It wasn't a very tall tree house because it was nestled in the trunk of a mimosa. He also built an attached ladder so I could easily climb up to it. When you got up there, you sat on a wide, flat board that was rimmed with two-by-fours all around the edges. Four corner posts held up another piece of plywood for a roof. It was painted white, and when I sat up there I could see all the way down the back alley and into the neighbors' yards.

I loved that tree house.

The only reason I wanted a tree house in the first place was because my friend, Jennifer, who lived around the corner had one, only I was too scared to climb up in it anymore.

Her tree house was in a huge tree by their driveway and it only consisted of a few boards nailed onto different limbs of the tree to help you move around a little more easily once you got up there. The tree was so tall that it needed a ladder to climb up to the lowest branch.

One day, after Jennifer and I had been sitting up there awhile, she decided to climb down and go into the house for some Popsicles. I assumed she was going to climb back up and we would eat them in the tree. When she came back outside she moved the ladder away from the tree and started laughing, telling me to come down and get my Popsicle. She kept laughing and sucking on her Popsicle while mine melted completely, because I wasn't about to attempt to shimmy down that tree trunk without the ladder. Finally I started crying loudly enough that her dad came outside and moved the ladder back so that I could get down.

That's why my tree house wasn't very tall and had an attached ladder.

There were lots of times in my life that I didn't believe that Daddy loved me. Or that he even liked me. But that tree house took a lot of work and I knew that.

Supper

One of my favorite times of the day is 5:30, watching the evening news while fixing supper. Something about being in the kitchen—feeding the dog, listening to the news, the smell, the heat, the sizzle, bubble, or crackle from whatever's cooking on the stove—takes me back to the embryonic warmth and safety of supper in a house on Speedway Avenue in Wichita Falls, Texas. During the seventeen years I lived in my parents' home, there were very few dinners we didn't eat together.

It was calm and quiet before the meal, with only the sound of my conversations with my mother about homework, what happened at school that day, and whatever was on TV. We listened to Chet Huntley and David Brinkley or we heard Walter Cronkite tell us, "That's the way it is." There were always pictures of fighting in Vietnam.

Mama fixed spaghetti, garlic bread, and salad or canned salmon croquettes with new potatoes and English peas. Red beans and cornbread with fried potatoes and sliced tomatoes. On Saturday nights when it was too cold for Daddy to grill outside and for us to eat at our picnic table on the patio, the hamburgers were cooked in the skillet, with so much pink in the middle that you expected them to moo. On a really good night there was dessert, like Scotch chocolate cake with icing chock full of coconut and crushed pecans. But nothing compared to my mom's homemade biscuits and sausage cream gravy for breakfast on a Saturday morning.

On Sunday nights we ate pancakes on TV trays in the den so we could watch *Bonanza* after church. We liked to make home-made ice cream and we invited other families over for dinner. We entertained my dad's Sunday school class and we had showers and luncheons for girls who were getting married or going off to college. We had a pantry full of food from the A & P and half of a side of beef in a deep freeze on the porch.

We thanked God before every meal. My father led the vast majority of those prayers, but when he wouldn't, my mother did. And in the summers, when I was home from school and we ate lunch without him, she and I took turns.

My job was to set the table, making sure the knife blade was facing the plate and the spoon was on the outside, and to fill the glasses with ice and pour the tea.

And when I was older I fixed the salad. I hated that job because all the vegetables were cold from having been in the crisper, and my fingertips got so cold they turned numb. But we had to have salad every night, my mother said, because it was part of a balanced meal. She knew, she always told me, because she had been a home economics major in college. And she had been cooking since she was twelve.

Mama set the cooking standard very high. She was a Martha Stewart before anyone had heard of Martha Stewart. Cooking seemed so easy for her. She knew exactly what to put together to make her dishes taste the same every time, and they were always good. Always. I never tasted anything my mother made that wasn't good. Any time we had a potluck meal at church, for example, it never seemed to be any trouble whatsoever for her to whip up something. And whatever my mom fixed always went fast.

When I was older my mom let me bake cookies, and I learned to make a mayonnaise chocolate cake, which sounds disgusting but was delicious. She taught me to go through a recipe and collect all your ingredients first, and to clean up your mess as you went along, to save time and to work more efficiently. She showed me how to rake the baking soda out of the box on the side so that you measured it precisely. And how to hold everything over the bowl so you didn't spill on the counter and have another mess to clean up.

I thought Mama knew everything. And I wanted to do things just like her. And to do them exactly the way she wanted me to. She had figured out the most cost-effective, time-saving, energy-preserving method to do anything, so the way she taught you to do it really was the best way. There were times where she'd take the spoon from me and say, "Here, just let me do it." She didn't say it in an ugly way, but what I heard was that I was taking too long and I wasn't doing it exactly like she wanted. That made me nervous. After a while, it was easier to let her do the cooking.

My world was filled with women cooking—all the women in my family could cook well—so the ability to cook and perform in the kitchen became a part of my little girl's picture of what it took to be a woman.

When the families got together for holidays, I preferred to stay out of the way. The women never told me to. They always had things for me to do, but I never felt comfortable doing them. It was easier and more enjoyable to go play with the boys. As I became an adult, my nervousness about being in the kitchen became even more embarrassing because I kept thinking, I'm supposed to know how to do this, but I don't. I wanted to be with them, but no matter how hard I tried, I could never keep up.

So at Thanksgiving and Christmas I made the salad and eventually got promoted to whipped cream.

Every night before we went to bed Mama fixed the coffee for the next morning in an electric percolator on the counter. I stood next to her, breathing deeply to catch the delicious aroma as she scooped grounds into the filter inside the percolator's metal basket and filled the pot with water. Then we'd turn out all the lights in the kitchen and go to bed.

It was always my mother who tucked me in, snuggled with me to read stories, kissed me good night, and brought me drinks of water when I wasn't really thirsty but simply prolonging the lights being turned out.

Sometimes she lay down with me because I had trouble falling asleep. When things weren't right with my dad, she slept all night with me. Even when things were right again, she often continued to stay with me. I was afraid a lot at night and I didn't like sleeping by myself, so I wanted her to stay, but somehow I also knew I was too old to still be sleeping with my mother. I didn't want the other kids at school to know. I was embarrassed. But not enough to stop.

Hospitality

Supposedly we didn't have a lot of money while I was growing up, but I never knew it. We never missed a meal, we lived in a nice house, even if it did have only one bathroom, and it was always a comfortable temperature inside. We went on vacations and there were two cars in our driveway. By a lot of standards, we were wealthy. My mom had taught school before I was born, but during the years before I started school, she stayed home with me. So we lived on my dad's salary, which was plenty to take care of what we needed, even if it meant we ate a lot of red beans and cornbread. And it took care of some other folks, too.

In many ways we were a very traditional American family. My dad mowed the yard and my mother cleaned the house and did the laundry. I had a birthday cake every year, along with a party, presents, and cards that my mother signed from "Mama and Daddy." I took piano lessons and they both came to my recitals. I played in the band and they both came to the concerts.

One of the sweetest lessons I learned from both my parents was their love for and generosity toward other people. My parents lived hospitality, even when it infringed on what might have been more convenient for us. Our door was always open, and people came for my mother's cooking, affection, and listening heart and they came for my father's playfulness and willingness to engage anyone who would participate in conversation. I watched my mom and dad make everyone feel welcome in our home. They were better at it than anyone I've ever known.

There were families at church in whom my parents took a special interest. Usually anyone who had less and needed help, those who didn't quite fit in, and especially families without fathers.

One such family's father had left after having an affair—something still considered scandalous in the 1960s, especially among church-going folk. Three of the four kids were teenagers when their dad left. The oldest son had been drafted into the army and was serving in Vietnam. The mother had no college education and had never worked outside their home, so they were having a hard time making ends meet. Sometimes they ate meals with us. At Christmas we had fun taking them presents, complete with snacks to eat while we all decorated the tree that we brought them.

Another family, a mother and three children, lived in government housing after their father had abandoned them. The oldest boy was in my father's Wednesday night class for the junior high boys at church. I was five when their mother became sick and died unexpectedly. My mom went to their house to serve a meal after the funeral, and I went with her. I played with the kids in the bedroom where they all three slept—the oldest daughter a freshman in high school, a son in the eighth grade, and another son in the sixth grade.

When my mom had finished serving the meal with the other ladies from church, and everything had been cleaned and put away, she came and told the three children to get their things together because they were going home with us.

After she saw the meager assortment of belongings they had gathered, she drove to Treasure City, a local discount store similar to Walmart, where she bought them toothbrushes and other toiletries as well as new clothes. When we got home, she called my dad at work and told him what she'd done.

While my mom had been serving dinner to the family, she asked them where the kids were going to live, assuming their father or their grandmother would take them. She was astounded to hear that neither of them planned to take the children, and even more so when they had no objection to her taking all three of them home to live with us. Mama didn't know exactly how my father would react to what she had done, but I think deep down she knew he had a heart for those kids—for any kid who grew up in a family that didn't want them. And they both knew it was the right thing to do.

We didn't have extra room for them, and it was more difficult to feed six people than it was to feed three, particularly when two of them were growing boys! But that didn't matter to my parents. For the next several months those kids lived with us in our two bedroom, one bathroom house. The boys slept on a sofa bed in the den, and the girl slept in my bed with me. She was fourteen and I was five. For the first time in my life I had older siblings.

I loved having them there, except for having to get up early and ride with my mother in my pajamas to take each of them to a different school. In the afternoons we picked them up. Every day, in between dropping them off and picking them up, we did laundry. And every day my mother washed the sheets from the sofa bed where the youngest boy wet the bed. Why wouldn't he, my mother said—his world had been turned upside down.

The children's mother had designated our church as the executor of her estate, meager as it was, so that meant the church leadership made the final decision about the children. Since their father refused to raise them, and no other relative wanted to take responsibility for them, the church decided to place them in a children's home. It was a sad day when we all piled in the car and drove to the place where those kids would live out what was left, if anything, of their childhood. For the next several years they alternated spending holidays with us and another family or two from church. After they were grown we lost touch with them. But for a while, my parents were Mom and Dad to those kids just like they were to me.

Through the years my parents took in others who didn't have anyone else to help them, families we bought groceries for, meals my mom prepared and served. I was shaped by their mentality that said you share what you have, you take care of people—especially those who have been forgotten and left behind—no matter what circumstances got them there.

The hospitality my parents frequently demonstrated revealed their true hearts. Those were life-shaping moments for a little girl who was learning what it meant to be a follower of Jesus.

Head Scarf

Whenever the temperature got below sixty degrees outside, my mother dressed me for the Klondikes. I looked like Ralphie's little brother in *A Christmas Story*. Even though for me, "walking to school in the wintertime" meant moving from the car to the school door—a distance of approximately ten feet—I still had to wear a coat, gloves, and a head scarf. If it looked like there might be a drizzle at any point during the day, I had to wear red rubber boots.

In first grade most kids wore stocking caps to keep their heads warm, but I had to wear a silk scarf tied around my head, just like my mother, now in her mid-forties, wore. She wore a scarf because she didn't want to mess up the perfectly coiffed, bouffant hairstyle typical of stylish women in the 1960s. You didn't spend all that time teasing your hair to get it to stand up that high only to have it flatten it out in one good gust of Texas wind. But my hair was flat anyway, straight as a board, in a pixie cut. Wearing a knit cap pulled down on my head probably would have kept my ears a lot warmer than that stupid silky scarf. My mother insisted though, and away we went to school.

I didn't like wearing it. None of the other girls in my first grade class wore anything remotely resembling a scarf. And worst of all, I didn't know how to tie it because my mother always tied it for me. So at the end of every school day when we kids got ready to go home, I'd go up to my teacher, Mrs. Simons, and ask her to tie it for me. I'd stand there wearing my coat, gloves, and rubber boots, and hold my chin up high so she'd have plenty of room to tie the scarf underneath. Then, like some Eastern European immigrant child, I'd waddle out to the sitter's car, parked ten feet from the door. When we went to recess outside, I bundled up in it. She told me that if I didn't, I'd get sick. And I was a good little girl. I did what my mother told me. Whether she was anywhere around or not. It made me nervous to even consider disobeying her.

One day as everyone was leaving school, I waited around to ask Mrs. Simons to tie my scarf. She and I were the only ones in the classroom. She sat down in one of our little chairs, positioned me right in front of her, and said, "Sally, I'm going to teach you how to tie this yourself. You're too smart not to know how to do this." I was a little embarrassed because I didn't know how, but really thrilled that she was teaching me. Even more thrilled that she thought I could do it myself. From then on, I never asked for help with the scarf again.

Sleepyhead

During my third and fourth grade years, it was easier for me to attend school where my mother taught second grade, so I transferred from our neighborhood school to hers. That meant I had to get up every weekday morning to make the flying trip across town to Jefferson Elementary School.

The problem is, I've always been a night person. There was—and still is—no such thing as a good morning if it means having to be somewhere before ten o'clock. So when my mother came to wake me for school, I was grumpy and pulled the covers over my head and just lay there. In the most loving voice imaginable, she began talking me awake and kissing me on the cheek. Her sweetness just made me grumpier.

She left the room for a few minutes, then returned to stand at my door and tell me in a firmer voice that it was time to get ready for school. Still, I stayed in bed. The next time she came back it wasn't so pleasant. At that point I got up.

Much to my mother's dismay, I also wasn't much of a breakfast eater. Every morning I'd hear the "breakfast is the most important meal of the day" lecture followed by the information that she had eaten bacon, eggs, and toast every day since she was a child. The only thing I would eat that early in the morning was a brown sugar and cinnamon Pop-Tarts or a cinnamon roll. If we were running late, which was often the case, my breakfast was a

Cap'n Crunch shake or Carnation Instant Breakfast. Chocolate flavored.

Mama drove faster on those trips to school than at any other time. And as I said, my mother never went anywhere slowly. Once we were in the car for the fifteen-minute ride across town, she started in on the next lecture of the morning. "You've got to get up earlier, Sally! Mama has a job and she has got to be at work at a certain time. I can't be late every day!"

The radio was always on in the car, and my mother's lecturing voice slowly faded into the background as I tuned her out to listen to Joe Tom White giving the KWFT farm report, followed by radio jingles from local businesses that I sang along with silently.

"Gibson's, Gibson's, I love to shop at Gibson's—
Gibson's Discount Center.
Where the discount touch means so much—
Every customer's a winner!
Gibson's built their reputation
On courtesy and consideration.
Save up to 50% on every item at Gibson's!"

II
The Lies Take Root

Riding Bicycles

Learning to ride a bicycle is one of those rites of passage for kids that gives a sense of independence that wasn't there before. One of the keys to riding a bike is learning to balance. I can't explain how it happens—how it is that you find that balance—you just do. You're riding along with someone you trust running behind you, holding onto the back of the seat to keep you steady, and then all of a sudden you realize they've let go and you're doing it on your own.

It took a lot longer than most for me to find that sense of balance.

Since I was an only child my mom didn't just turn me loose to go play. Now she acknowledges that she might have been somewhat overprotective. Okay, very overprotective. I'm telling you, being raised to be conscious of the thousands of ways you could get hurt in any given situation made great "worst case scenario" training for me as a personal injury litigator, but as a little kid, it's anxiety producing and exhausting. You expend so much energy worrying about hurting yourself, you miss out on just having fun. You end up being scared of everything, and so you don't play with other kids as much. Of course, you don't have as many experiences getting stitches in emergency rooms, either.

I wanted to be able to do things like the other kids. When they had skating parties, I couldn't skate. When they had swimming parties, I couldn't swim. And when it came to playground equipment, like merry-go-rounds and jungle gyms, ladders and see-saws, well, I didn't much care for those either. I was the biggest scaredy-cat around, but I couldn't let on that I was afraid, or kids would make fun of me. I knew that if I acted nonchalant, as though I couldn't care less, kids would leave me alone. But that was part of the problem—kids left me alone.

Mama always said she focused on the important things, the things that last. Although I learned many good, eternal things from her, it's also important for a kid to feel like she fits in. Because even nice kids don't know what to do with a kid who can't skate, swim, or ride a bike. And the not-so-nice ones laugh.

If I hadn't so desperately wanted to fit in I never would've learned to do any of that typical kid stuff. Especially riding a bike. I didn't mind that I didn't know how to ride, but other kids talked about it and it looked like fun.

In second grade I confided to a friend that I didn't know how to ride a bicycle. Instead of being helpful, she laughed and threatened to tell everyone in our class unless I kissed her pet chameleon that she'd bought at our elementary school's fall festival. Sitting on the bed in her bedroom, I watched that bright green lizard slinking around, a red string tied around its neck like a dog's leash, and I thought, how disgusting. I might not have been able to do all the things kids are supposed to know how to do, but I certainly wasn't stupid enough to even think about kissing that lizard, so I said, "Go ahead. Tell."

The next day at school my friend was going to "out" me during show and tell. Before she had a chance, I did a skit that I'd seen on *The Dean Martin Show*, and everybody thought it was funny. My teacher thought it was funny enough to send me upstairs with a note to have the teacher let me perform it for her sixth grade class. Sorta stole my classmate's thunder.

———————— ✦ ————————

My first bicycle was turquoise blue with dipped chrome handlebars and the coolest metallic turquoise banana seat. It still had the training wheels on it when Daddy brought it home from work when I was eight. I rode it around in circles on our patio because that's the only place I had to ride. We lived on the corner of a major intersection and there weren't any sidewalks. There weren't a lot of kids to play with, and being that our street was a major thoroughfare, the kids that did live on my street didn't play much in their front yards. So I kept riding around on the patio with the training wheels on my bike. For three more years.

The secret to learning to ride a bicycle is that the person holding on to the back of the bike has to let go. And sometimes you fall. You might fall quite a few times before you get the hang of it. But the only way to learn is for the person running behind you to give up trying to prevent you from ever falling. To stop running behind you and simply stand there, firmly planted, and watch you ride off down the driveway by yourself. Sure, if they let go too soon, you'll fall, and maybe you'll be too afraid to try again. But if they hold on too long, you will never learn to do it on your own. Then you start to wonder if you really can do it. Even worse is believing that you might not ever be able to do it at all without the person running behind you. And you become perfectly content not to try at all.

Family Affair

There was a warmth and a sweetness, a calmness and security about my early years in our first house that I can still feel, and at times in my life I've searched diligently to recreate that. At the same time, some of my most horrible memories happened in that house.

In my family we watched TV more than we ate, and that's saying a lot. TV had only been around for about a decade when I came along, and having a TV set was still fairly new to my parents, so it was especially entertaining. Most of our evenings were spent together watching TV.

One of my favorite shows as a first grader was *Family Affair*, about three orphaned children who come to live with their bachelor uncle in his high-rise New York City apartment. I loved watching Buffy and Jody, the red-haired twins who were about the same age as me, being loved and taken in by their uncle when their parents were killed in a car accident. And even though Mr. French, Uncle Bill's butler, acted perturbed that he had to take care of them, he came to love them, too. Buffy had a doll named Mrs. Beasley who had curly, bright yellow locks and was dressed in a bright blue, yellow polka dotted dress. And she wore glasses. Mattel must've made a killing from that show because every little girl I knew had a Mrs. Beasley doll in the late 1960s. So did I.

One night I changed into my cotton pajamas with the tiny pink and blue sheep print and snap buttons. Mama had recently cut the pajama bottoms into shorts because it was now springtime and my legs had grown too long for them anyway. I'd worn them a lot, so they were soft and comfy. I turned on the TV and lay down on the couch as the *Family Affair* theme song came on.

My parents were still in their bedroom changing into their pajamas before coming to the den to watch TV with me before we all went to bed. I could hear their voices coming from their bedroom, way back in the other part of the house. It sounded as if they were laughing and playing, so I got up and started toward their room, not wanting to be left out of the fun. It wasn't until I got to the middle of the hallway that led into their bedroom that I realized they weren't playing.

My heart stopped as I looked through the doorway.

Daddy was screaming at my mother, wielding a yardstick, waving it as though he might hit her. His face was white as a sheet and his eyes seemed to bulge out of his head. Over and over again he screamed, "Don't you ever call me a coward, do you hear!?" His words were thick and strong and ugly. He used other awful words that I knew were cursing.

Mama stood on her side of the bed next to her closet, trying to grab the yardstick out of Daddy's hand when he swung it at her. Even when he turned and saw me standing in the doorway, he didn't stop swinging the yardstick and screaming and cursing at her.

Not much taller than the yardstick, I ran to my mother and wrapped my arms around her leg, burying my face in her thigh. I had already learned that my crying provoked Daddy, but I couldn't help it. I was absolutely terrified.

Mama kept trying to grab the yardstick, pleading, "Don't hurt this baby! Don't hurt this baby!"

Nothing stopped him. To little Sally, it seemed as if his terrifying rage was directed at her. Even after Mama picked me up and ran out of the bedroom, he followed us, cursing all the way down the hallway. She took me into the living room and held me on the couch, my father still yelling at us.

Finally the storm ceased, as unpredictably as it had begun, and Daddy disappeared.

I clung to the safety of my mother's arms in the darkness.

"Shhh," she said, her mouth by my ear and speaking oh so quietly so Daddy wouldn't hear and the raging start all over again. "We have to think of this as though that wasn't really Daddy. He's not in his right mind when he acts like that. That man looks like Daddy, but it's not really him."

I kept my face buried in her shoulder. I couldn't cry. I couldn't move. I held still, as though that would take away what just happened.

"Honey, we can't tell anyone." She leaned back and brushed my hair from my eyes so she could look into them. "People wouldn't understand, Sally, so we shouldn't say anything. There are some close friends who know he throws fits like that, but they can't do anything, and knowing about it just upsets them. Anybody else might not believe us." She rocked a little, cupping my head in her hand, holding me tight again. "It would hurt Papa and Mammy if they knew, so you can't tell them either." She pulled away to look at me again. "Do you understand, Sally? Nobody. We can't tell anyone."

I nodded. "A secret?"

"Yes, Sally. A secret."

"Just for us, Mama?"

"Just for us."

She held me as she sang the song she had sung so many times before, and I fell asleep to the familiar words that had already been speaking eternal truth into my growing heart.

Though the way we journey may be often drear,
We shall see the King some day.
On that blessed morning,
Clouds will disappear,
We shall see the King some day!

I don't know when I went to bed. I only know that my mother slept with me that night, and the next morning I got up, dressed, and went to school as though nothing had happened.

I don't think I was ever more afraid than I was that night. It's one of my earliest, most vivid memories. I think a part of me died that night. I know my world changed. One minute I was on the couch, feeling completely safe, listening to calliope music, looking forward to a fun show about kids on TV. The next I'm witnessing something terrifying that will change my perspective on life for years to come.

I wish I could forget. But even now, as I write about it, the memories conjure up the same racing heart, dry mouth, chills, and shakes that come with fright.

Daddy had had other bouts of rage before that time, but I don't remember those except in snippets and snapshots as though they were clipped from a dream. And there were many that followed it. His outburst, like all of them over the years to come, seemed to come out of nowhere.

If you see the signs of danger approaching, like a tornado in the distance, or the glowing heat of a fire in a wood stove, you can avoid the burn altogether. But when you have no way of predicting that danger, but know it could happen at any time, without any warning whatsoever, well, that's the worst.

A child doesn't have a way to process the unpredictable. Knowing that violence can occur so randomly, and without warning, shapes the way you think about the safety of your home and the world.

Living in fear changes the way you feel. And it changes the way you think.

I spent much of my life trying to minimize this scene. I never witnessed my father hit my mother, and he never, ever hit me. But I grew up believing he might. And living with the fear of that possibility took its toll.

Twenty-five years later I was cleaning my house one Saturday afternoon with the TV playing in the background. Unexpectedly, calliope music began to play—the theme song from *Family Affair*. I dropped the dust rag, curled up in a ball on the couch in my living room, and sobbed uncontrollably. That was the first sign—at least the first sign I recognized—that I needed help.

Separation

Daddy tried to be extra helpful around the house or bought me presents to make up for getting mad and throwing fits. One time he brought me a toy gun holster with a revolver that I loved. It looked like Matt Dillon's on *Gunsmoke*. Another time he brought home that bicycle with the turquoise blue banana seat and plastic tassels hanging off the handlebars. Building my treehouse was another of his peace offerings.

A story I used to comfort and give myself hope was the one my mom told about the night my dad walked down the aisle to be baptized. The story reassured me that somewhere inside of this angry person was the man I wanted to be my father and call Daddy. The man I longed to be close to. A man whose heart was touched by the Christ I was already being drawn to as a little girl. The song that had touched my daddy that morning, Mama said, was a hymn we still sang at invitation time.

"Years I spent in vanity and pride,
Caring not my Lord was crucified.
Knowing not it was for me he died,
On Cal-va-ry!
Mercy, there was grace and grace was free –
Pardon, there was multiplied to me.
There, my burdened soul found liberty
At Cal-va-ry!"

Whenever we sang that song in church I watched him try to hide the tears behind his black horn-rimmed glasses. How I longed to reach over and take his hand. Touch his arm. Acknowledge that I was thankful for those words, and that they touched me, too. Even if I couldn't yet fathom the depths of that mercy, I knew there was something powerful that touched my daddy's heart. Instead, I sat between my mother's welcoming presence and a father who seemed very far away.

Oh, how I wanted to lose the hesitance, the doubt, the fear, that at any moment I could unknowingly do something to trigger Daddy's rage and we would go back to the place I despised! The place where only his body remained and a man I feared more than anything occupied his skin. At those times I saw no compassion in him, no tenderness, no playfulness. We were left with a man who was silent and detached at best, and volatile and cruel at his worst. I missed my daddy during those awful times.

As I got older, with each fit of Daddy's rage, I went through a spectrum of emotions ranging from fear to apathy to hopelessness. At first I was simply petrified with a heart-racing, heart-pounding fear that caused my mouth to get dry and to stutter if I tried to speak. My whole body shook, as though a fever's chill had come over me. I was afraid to go into another part of the house because I feared what he might do to my mother if I wasn't there. So I sat on the sofa, motionless, expressionless, and listened to the venom. When he had stopped raging—maybe by the next hour, the next day, maybe longer—I felt numb, as though nothing had happened.

My mother acted as though nothing had happened, probably in an attempt to maintain some type of normalcy for me. She woke me for school, got herself ready, fixed breakfast, cleaned it all up, fed the dog, and drove us to school. She taught at school all day, came home by way of the grocery and drug stores, and ran any other errands. At home she fixed supper, talked to me and listened to all the stories of my day at school. She fed the dog, cleaned up the dishes, graded papers, created lesson plans while watching TV and talking to me, called her mother to check on her, and talked to people from the church on the phone. She kept going, no matter what happened. So I did, too.

My father would come home from work, and without speaking to my mother or me, change his clothes, sit at the table I had set, eat in silence the food my mother had prepared, ignore my mother and me as we talked, take his plate to the sink when he finished, and retreat to his study. He sat in the dark, listening to a ballgame on the radio, or paying bills in the light of a desk lamp. He sat at the same desk where, on Saturday nights, he studied the Sunday school lesson he would teach the following morning. Then he got up, and without telling my mother or me goodnight, changed into his pajamas and crawled into bed.

When my father emotionally separated himself from us, I hated needing to use the bathroom. To get there, I had to go right past the study. I tried not to look, but I could see him sitting in the dark. I felt a strange mixture of fear and sadness. Fear of doing something to trigger his anger, but sadness to see him all alone. I was confused over what had made him mad, so I figured it was best to tiptoe by, not doing or saying anything that might upset him. But oh, how I hated walking right by the door as though he wasn't there.

I would've given anything to feel the freedom to crawl up on his lap and hug him and cry until there were no tears, but I had to be emotionless, expressing nothing that I felt. So I went to the bathroom as quietly and unobtrusively as I could, flushed the commode, and bolted past his door, back down the hall to the safety of the den and my mother.

I didn't dare let him see how angry I was after one of his episodes. Anger that came from being afraid and from the unfairness of it all, yet with no way to express those feelings. As a very little girl, the only safe way I found to express my anger was how I set his place at the table. Instead of neatly folding the napkin and placing his silverware just so, as I usually did at each of our plates, I simply pitched his silverware onto the placemat, not caring if the knife blade was facing the plate as I had been taught. Any greater expression of disapproval was too risky.

Growing up in the midst of all that, I acquired the survival skill of pretending that what happened wasn't that bad, yet hurting more deeply than I was ever allowed to express. I learned to cry without making a sound. I got so good at hiding my emotions that I eventually became totally unaware of what I was really feeling. I learned to be exactly who I needed to be to please the people around me, and in doing so, I believed that would make everything better. And maybe, just maybe, Daddy would like me.

There were too many days that my father lived in the same house as me, walked past me and sat at the dinner table with me, and never said a word to me.

As though I weren't there.

As though I didn't exist.

Trust?

Daddy hadn't even turned off the ignition when Mama started.

"Now Dan," she said, "you hold onto her. Don't let her go."

I dropped back from my usual spot of hanging over the front seat and slumped out of sight.

"And don't get upset if Sally gets scared."

"I know what to do, Betty." Daddy yanked the keys out of the ignition. "Good grief, I'm not completely stupid."

I grabbed my beach towel and slid across the seat to let myself out. By the age of nine, this conversation had become common. One where Mama instructed Daddy, and he'd respond in protest—sounding much like the pre-pubescent boy she was addressing. And I knew everyone was upset because of me.

The car door slammed and I jumped, tensing inside, not knowing if Daddy would explode or just stay annoyed. I could never figure out whether he was more annoyed with my mother or with me for being such a baby.

Because my mom told my dad the same things over and over, to "be patient, don't let go of her," and not to do this or not to do that, I believed that men must be incredibly stupid.

That's not at all what my mother meant as she spoke to my dad. She had good reason to be unsure how he would react to me in any given situation, because she couldn't figure out what provoked his anger either. There had been too many times when he had been unpredictable. Unsafe.

A child's perception and interpretation of events, especially while observing those occurring between adults, often isn't accurate. For example, I believed Daddy didn't care as much for me as Mama did, even though I was his little girl, too. And when he became frustrated with my fears, I interpreted his irritation to mean that he didn't want to be with me. If we had to go through all this hassle to get in the water, ride a roller coaster or ski lift, or to go through a haunted house, why would he want to do anything with me? Little girls were "scaredy cats," as the boys at school taunted over and over.

I tucked my rolled-up towel underneath my arm as Mama had taught me, trying to block their angry words at each other. I kicked at some pebbles with my shoe, thinking that if I could be more like the boys, like my cousins, maybe I wouldn't be as much trouble and my dad would like me more.

Boys weren't afraid of anything. They didn't have to be.

In a child's world, the more consistent a parent's responses, the more predictable the parent, the safer and less anxious the child feels. If a child gets her hand swatted every time she reaches to touch the stove, she learns not to do that; she knows what to expect. If every time a certain subject is broached and her dad gets riled, she learns not to bring that up. But if there's no rhyme or reason to his reactions it's confusing at the least and emotionally disabling at its worst.

Anne Lamott in her book *Traveling Mercies* says, "This is how you induce psychosis in rats: you behave inconsistently with them; you keep changing the rules. One day when they press down the right lever, expecting a serving of grain like they've always gotten before, they instead get a shock. And eventually the switching back and forth drives them mad, while the rats who get shocked every time they press the lever figure it out right away and work around it" (p.19).

When I was a little girl Daddy's eruptions happened frequently. By the time I was in middle school, he might rage only once a year. In a way, though, that was worse. I was baffled trying to figure out what to expect from one minute to the next. He could be the most fun, playful person, acting silly and telling jokes. He'd be talking to me and playing catch with me in the backyard one day, and the next, something would've set him off into a rage and he wouldn't even acknowledge that I existed. No matter how hard I tried, I could never predict the precise moment he would erupt. I was always stunned, always shocked that it had happened again. I was like the rat where the rules changed without warning. I was always waiting for that electric shock. Always.

There were times when I'd hear a conversation escalate and feel my stomach tie into knots, knowing what was coming. I wanted to say, "Please stop, Mama. Please don't say anything or he'll get mad again. Let it go, it doesn't matter. Let him do it the way he wants. It'll be okay." That stomach-wrenching dance could go on for days or even weeks.

Each time it became harder and harder to trust and love and be close again. Each time I prayed and wished and hoped—and worst of all, believed—that he would never do it again. But in a heartbeat we were back and he was thrashing us with words again. In his most hateful rages he told me I was nothing but a spoiled brat. When I grew older he called me a bitch. Each bout of rage killed a deeper part of my soul as sadness and terror wove together deep inside me. A thick callous of shame grew around me.

Once when I was fourteen and had taken hours of his venom, I lashed back. Not to excuse it, but after all, I was fourteen. Within the hour I became convinced that it was all my fault and I hesitantly approached him at his desk to apologize. He turned on me again, rising from his desk, his eyes bulging with anger.

I think that was when a part of me shut down. I stopped believing that he might ever be different, that these fits of rage and periods of total emotional absence would ever end. I felt so stupid for forgiving him each time, for wanting to be close to him so much that I would pretend nothing had happened.

A stranger living in our home would have, at the very least, exchanged cordial greetings and small talk with me. My father didn't speak, didn't even look at me. Then maybe after several days, a week, weeks, after I had said every day, "Hi, Daddy," when he came home from work, one day he'd break the silence.

"Hi, Sal."

And my heart leapt.

Then he looked at my mother and said hello.

She responded with a curt hello, never looking up from fixing dinner. Since my mother never moved an inch toward him, I didn't either.

But oh, how I wanted to.

At that point it didn't matter what he'd said, what he'd done, how badly he'd frightened me or threatened us. None of it mattered because he was coming back. He was at least speaking again. I wanted to bolt to him and throw my arms around his waist and kiss him like we always did when we weren't in this horrible place.

Mama made it clear we weren't supposed to act like everything was okay until he apologized. I guess it was good to teach a little girl that when you explode you need to make it right and apologize. Otherwise I might have grown up thinking it was okay for men to treat women and children that way, and gotten into an abusive relationship with a man myself.

I had to do as my mother wanted, because I depended on her for everything, my safety included. But after a few weeks of living with my father's silence—an eternity to a child—I just wanted my daddy. I didn't care if he said all the right words first.

Over the next few days, or sometimes weeks, my father would slowly return. As though he had been gone on a trip and now he was back and readjusting to being part of the family again. He rejoined us at the dinner table and tried to enter the conversations that had never stopped between my mother and me. He sat in the living room after supper and watched TV with us.

I could talk to him, but not completely, not freely, because things were still very distant between my mother and him. And I had to follow her lead. At some point my mother talked with my dad, explained the things he'd said that were so hurtful, and how he couldn't treat us like that. My mother was the best preacher I knew.

My father wept and said how sorry he was. At that point I was allowed to enter the room, but I never got to say how I had felt. I never got to say how hurt and scared and angry I was.

Desperately Seeking Daddy

Going somewhere with a man, even as a little girl, feels different than going somewhere with a woman. You learn that men do things differently and that it's not necessarily bad or not as good as the way a woman might do something—it's just different. And some things you like more. Like the way your hand feels so small in theirs. And how you can sit on their shoulders and see over everybody else.

The truth is, no matter how scared, no matter how angry, no matter how hesitant I was around my father, I still wanted to do things with him. I wanted to be like him. I wanted to be close to him. And why wouldn't I believe that was possible? All my mother ever talked about was how close she had been to her father, my papa. I had experienced that closeness with Papa for a few short years. I saw other little girls with their fathers at church or on TV, and they seemed to be close to their fathers, too. Why didn't I feel that with mine? I figured it was my fault. And if it was my fault, I had to fix it. I decided to do anything to get him to like me, and tried to be interested in what he liked.

He always played with my cousins who were boys, so I figured out early on that he liked things boys liked, so I tried to play the things they liked to play. But that rarely worked. Sports not only bored me, but I was terrible at them. One thing I learned was the best way to get his undivided attention was to play catch with him in the backyard. My mother always instructed him not to throw the ball too hard, telling him it would hurt my hand. He was, and it did, and after she told him to be gentle, he threw it even harder. I didn't care because we were doing something together.

Swimming would have been one place we could have connected if I hadn't been so afraid. However, despite that fear, I was thrilled to spot the swimming pool at motels where we'd stop while on vacation. I couldn't wait to go swimming with my dad, feeling a combination of excitement and nervousness. Well, we didn't actually go swimming. It was more like standing around in the shallow end of the pool. But when I was with him in the water I felt the deepest physical connection with him. My fear prompted me to cling to him in a way that I wasn't able to do on dry land. I relished what it felt like to be close to him. To feel the water on his skin, to see the water droplets on his nose and feel his prickly beard. Affection toward me didn't come easily for him. Sure, he hugged me. He kissed me. But it always felt awkward. So the only time I got the kind of physical closeness I greatly needed was in the water.

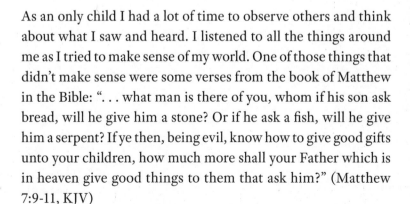

As an only child I had a lot of time to observe others and think about what I saw and heard. I listened to all the things around me as I tried to make sense of my world. One of those things that didn't make sense were some verses from the book of Matthew in the Bible: ". . . what man is there of you, whom if his son ask bread, will he give him a stone? Or if he ask a fish, will he give him a serpent? If ye then, being evil, know how to give good gifts unto your children, how much more shall your Father which is in heaven give good things to them that ask him?" (Matthew 7:9-11, KJV)

The verses didn't make sense because I knew they were meant to teach me about the goodness of God as Father. About how much God desired to give me good gifts even more than my earthly father wanted to. Yet my earthly father threw the ball too hard. He gave me presents after he'd been mean and cruel. He might give me something other than what I expected or what was good for me. Sometimes out of neglect. Sometimes as a joke.

Like the time we were in Florida in a souvenir shop where they had those fake brandy snifters that looked like they were filled with liquid, only when you turned them upside down, the liquid stayed inside. I wasn't quite two when he handed one to me and thought it was funny when I tried to turn it up and get a drink, only to discover nothing came out. Or when he poured a glass of buttermilk and gave me a drink, telling me it was regular milk. I'd sputter and spew because I couldn't stand the taste of buttermilk.

My dad retold those stories and thought they were funny. My mother told them with a tone of disapproval. I learned more from the telling than I did from the actual events.

I was always desperately seeking my daddy. But no matter what I did, no matter how hard I tried, I could never close the distance between us. Then, to make things even more confusing, there were the rare times when he could be safe and reassuring and not be bothered in the least.

There was the Halloween haunted house that all the other fourth graders were talking about at school. I didn't want to look like a big baby so I decided to go. I wanted my daddy to go with me and he did. And he never let go of me the whole time. He held my hand or he let me stand behind him and hold onto him. He made jokes going through the house and acted silly so I'd know it wasn't real and didn't have to be afraid. In that moment he did what a daddy was meant to do—without my mom telling him.

Or when I was learning to drive. He was far more patient with me behind the wheel than my mother.

Like the time when I'd had my license two months and I backed the car out of the driveway into a parked car across the street. And two weeks later backed our station wagon full of eleven teenagers into a telephone pole.

He never lost his cool. I never heard about the events again.

As I grew older, I took every moment Daddy gave me as a sign that he might like me. For example, he taught me to play tennis at the courts up the street from us. He knew how to put "the English" on the ball, making it appear as though it was going to land in one spot, but then, like magic, bounce backward. It frustrated me, but he taught me how to anticipate the move. He did the same thing when he played ping pong with me.

My dad never let me win at anything—tennis, ping pong, cards—so I knew that when I did, I'd truly accomplished something. And I learned to play well. But oddly, I often felt I was playing with an older brother who couldn't let himself look bad by losing to a girl.

I desperately wanted to know my daddy's stories like I knew my mother's, but he didn't often share things with us. I wanted to hear all those little details and stories of his growing up years—who he hung out with, what it was like to move around all the time, but especially how he learned to make that tennis ball change direction. I wanted to know about his life now.

I missed out on so much by not hearing how he thought and felt and what he experienced. The things you know about your parents from experience and from their stories that you hear over and over, are the things that set you up for life, for what you think about other people, for what you think about yourself.

I often wondered why my dad didn't participate in the routine aspects of raising me. I suppose part of the reason was the era. Men didn't commonly take part in child care, at least the day-to-day feeding and grooming that fathers are more prone to share with mothers today. In the 1960s, taking care of kids was left to women—at home, at church, everywhere.

Today my heart leaps when I see men at church taking their babies out of the assembly on a Sunday morning, diaper bag slung over a shoulder. I think something precious happens in those moments of caring for the physical needs of a child. And in those sacred moments of dad fixing the peanut-butter-and-jelly sandwich for his child or brushing her hair or putting on little shoes and socks a child learns there's another person besides Mom who really cares about her.

I suppose there's another reason for my dad not participating more—because Mama wanted to be the one to care for me. And if we're telling the truth, she has a certain way she likes things done, and if you don't do it that way, well, you're not doing it right. I think her constant correction and instruction upset my dad and he eventually quit trying.

I interpreted Daddy's lack of involvement as not caring as much about me as my mother did. It contributed to my belief that men were incapable of caring for a child's basic needs. Only women could do that. All three of those beliefs were lies.

Those particular lies were solidified the week before my papa died when I was in the second grade. Papa was dying of stomach cancer and my mother took off work and drove twenty-five miles to the small town where he lived in order to spend every minute at the hospital with him. Instead of me staying with my dad, my mom made arrangements for me to stay with family friends. I was utterly miserable.

It felt as though my whole world had come to an end. My papa whom I loved dearly was sick, my mother was gone, and I believed my daddy didn't want me. Only my mother wanted me. Only my mother was capable of caring for me, so if she wasn't there I had to go elsewhere, away from my family.

Of course I know now that wasn't the truth. But at seven, it made no sense, why I had to go stay with other people when my father remained in town, staying at our house, going home every night like he always did.

Why couldn't I stay there with him? My dad could've picked me up from the sitter's and maybe we could've gone to get hamburgers for supper. Or eaten at Luby's cafeteria. And maybe we could've sat in the den watching TV until it was time to go to bed. Daddy could've tucked me in and kissed me goodnight. And I would have been right where I belonged.

The Honeymoon

My parents often told a story from their honeymoon at parties or at dinner with friends, a story everyone thought was funny and made them laugh hysterically. I never did think it was funny, and it became less funny the more I heard it.

My mother always told the story while my father sat there and laughed along with everyone else. The more people laughed, the more they played it up like a comedy routine where men are made out to be thoughtless boobs and women have to take care of everything. Whether my mother embellished the story or not, it laid a foundation for what I came to believe about honeymoons, marriage, and relationships between men and women.

The story started out nice enough. They spent their honeymoon in Monterey, Mexico, and on the way back home, they stopped at a restaurant in the border town across from Laredo, Texas. The restaurant had been recommended to them by some friends as a swanky place that served all sorts of exotic game, including elk, pheasant, and quail. Only the meal was a little too exotic and they both came down with food poisoning, striking my mother first, in the middle of the night. She got up, sick as a dog, while my father lay in bed, not moving a muscle to care for her.

"Then," she'd say, "when I was finally able to get back in bed, did Dan ask if I was all right? Did he ask me if I needed anything? Did he offer to do anything? No. He rolls over, half asleep, and says . . . ." Then she'd imitate Daddy asking her in a whiney voice, "'What time is it?'"

"I can't believe how dumb I was for actually getting up to look at the clock to answer him, when I'm the one who was sick and the clock was on the nightstand next to his side of the bed!"

The next day the food poisoning hit my dad and he was too sick to drive. My mother was still sick, but she drove them to a pharmacy where she bought some Pepto-Bismol. My dad tried to tell her that he can't take liquid medicine, that it will make him throw up more. But she insisted. He gave in. He was right. It did make him sick. All over the dashboard.

My mom then drove across the border to a service station where she asked the service station attendant for help cleaning up the inside of the car.

It's at this point, while listening to my mother innocently explain to the service station attendant in great detail that she and her husband have contracted some stomach bug or food poisoning while on their honeymoon, that my father gets tickled. He starts laughing, despite his own sickness. He watches the service station attendant's expression as he patiently listens to my mom's story, and he realizes the attendant thinks that the vomiting is a result of getting drunk. He's not about to clean up the car for my mom as she sincerely believes he'll do.

"So you see, sir, we've been so sick. Would you please clean up the car for us?"

"No, lady, but there's a bucket of water over there and some paper towels that you can use," the attendant tells my mom, with a chuckle that meant, "You've got to be kidding me, lady."

Everybody listening to the story is laughing their hardest by now.

She comes back to the car, as indignant as Lucy Ricardo, saying, "Well, I never!" and tells my dad they're going to have to clean up the car themselves. Again, she imitates my father in a whiney voice declaring he can't help clean up the car or he'll be sick again, so she has to clean up the car by herself.

All the while my mom is telling this story, my dad's laughter is building. The more he laughs, the more all the people listening laugh, and the more they laugh, the more my mom exaggerates the voices and the more she expresses irritation for my dad.

While I'm watching both of them, I can't tell if his laughter is more out of embarrassment at his behavior, or if he really thought it was funny that she got stuck having to do everything.

The sad thing is, I didn't hear the stories about their wedding as much. They didn't get the wedding pictures out and talk about how happy they were the night of their wedding and tell the story of running away from their friends who had intended to kidnap Daddy on the wedding night as much as they told the story of being sick.

When I was eight years old I came home from school one day to find my mother sick with a migraine headache, unable to move out of bed without being nauseous. I sat on the bed with her, trying to be completely still so the movement wouldn't make her dizzy or nauseated. When my father came home he stood in the door of the bedroom and said, "If I were that sick, I'd get up and go to the doctor." Without acknowledging my presence, he turned and walked back down the hall to the kitchen and fixed himself something to eat.

These stories made me wonder if this is just the way men act. Is this the way husbands treat their wives? Is that what it means in Scripture when it says that husbands are to love their wives as Christ loves the church? That was confusing to me.

When I was in the sixth grade, I went to a slumber party and noticed something really different. The parents of the girl who was hosting the party were leisurely conversing in the father's study. They were discussing politics, and I couldn't help but eavesdrop. I was fascinated by their obvious enjoyment of talking to one another about something outside the family, their obligation to children, and maintaining a home. They were sharing a mutual interest in something that drew them together. While all the other little girls were running around getting popsicles to take outside to eat on the patio, I stood there mesmerized by this man and woman who genuinely enjoyed each other's company.

Some of the relationships between men and women and in families that I saw on TV and in movies looked nice. But I had real-life pictures of relationships between husbands and wives that more closely resembled Ralph and Alice Kramden on *The Honeymooners* or Archie and Edith Bunker on *All In the Family*. What I saw were pictures of men often being calloused to their wives' needs and feelings. While the female characters were smarter, they were often mistreated in those relationships. Most of the humor of these TV shows was lost on a little girl not yet old enough to grasp the concept of irony. What I did understand was the ineptitude of the male characters in both of those shows.

In my own home, it seemed we never shared a meal together that my mom didn't bring to attention that Daddy had spilled something on the table or down his shirt, or was crunching too loudly, or eating too fast. My mom loved to quote Philippians 4:8 which says to talk about things that are good, and positive, and encouraging, and yet when it came to my dad, she had fallen into this cycle of being so hurt, becoming so bitter, that it was almost impossible to find anything good to say. Over the years, her words, her tone, her facial expressions became increasingly critical. It was difficult to watch the vicious cycle of pain, unforgiveness, and growing resentment between two people who are supposed to love each other.

The stories I heard, the things I observed on TV and in real life, coupled with my own experience living with my parents, created a picture of marriage that was confusing at best, horrifying at its worst. Even as a little girl they led me to question the goodness and the benefits of marriage. If that was what marriage was like, who would want to enter into something like that? Especially if it was for the rest of your life, like the Bible said it was supposed to be. Being married meant that if you were female, you lost yourself and gained nothing in return.

And in my world, not only was marriage not happy, at times it was downright scary. I knew from the beginning that "happily ever after" was only in fairy tales.

Surgery

I was sick a lot as a kid. Lots of colds. Colds that turned into sinus infections. It got so bad that by my seventh-grade year they discovered I had a sinus cavity full of nasal polyps. I had surgery and discovered that the culprit all along had been severe allergies. I was allergic to the earth and everything in it. I felt like a cross between Felix Unger on *The Odd Couple* and that whiney Howard Sprague character on the color versions of *The Andy Griffith Show*. Both of those guys were always complaining about their allergies, and it was a source of a lot of laughter on both shows. I felt the same, especially the summer after my surgery when I had to wear earplugs and a nose clip when I got anywhere near the water.

The surgery was just something else that made me different from the other kids and made my mother more prone to hover. Her attention and over-protectiveness embarrassed me, but I didn't dare say anything about it. I didn't want to hurt her feelings. And I couldn't take the chance of being too independent. It was risky. More and more I came to believe that my very survival depended solely on her—that without her I wouldn't be able to do anything.

The night before my first surgery, at the age of twelve, I sat on my parents' bed and asked my mother to stay with me at the hospital. I asked her not to leave me, and she told me that she wouldn't. She kept her promise. Even though I was only supposed to be in the hospital one night, there were complications, and she ended up sleeping in a recliner in my room for the next four nights until I was able to go home. It didn't surprise me that she stayed. What did surprise me was the way my dad took care of me, too.

As much as I hated the whole ordeal of the surgery and being in the hospital, one of my grossest memories in my life is also the sweetest. To understand how much the experience meant to me you have to first know that I had never experienced my father caring for my physical needs. He didn't prepare meals or snacks for me and he never participated in helping me get dressed. He wasn't the one who got up with me when I had bad dreams in the middle of the night. He didn't take my temperature or bring me medicine when I was sick. I don't even remember him driving me to school or taking me to dentist or doctor appointments.

My surgery had been more extensive than the doctor had anticipated, lasting four hours. I had lost a lot of blood and ingested most of it, and they had packed my sinuses so I could only breathe through my mouth. As I began to rouse from the anesthesia, I was violently nauseated and began vomiting uncontrollably before I was fully awake.

It was miserable. As confused as I was, one thing became very clear. Each time I opened my eyes during the sick spells I saw my father's hands holding the pan for me to throw up in. At home, whenever I had a stomach virus, my dad ran from the room, insisting he couldn't be around anyone vomiting or it would make him sick, too. My mother was the one who held my head over the commode, wiping my face with a wet washcloth. But there, in the worst moment of sickness I'd ever experienced, stood my dad right beside my bed, holding the pan and not budging. I never heard him complain or say one thing about how gross it was to be there with me.

Maybe that's not a big deal to a lot of people. Maybe their fathers did that all the time. But the fact that mine did that for me, well, that was a big deal. It was hard for him.

The sad thing is, I wanted to keep on throwing up if it meant I could feel that sense of closeness and caring from him.

There was something strangely symbolic about that night, lying in that hospital bed, sick as a dog, feeling absolutely miserable, not being able to breathe, and yet so content. My mom stood on one side of my bed, caring for me, and on the other side was my dad. They were working in sync with each other and there was no bickering or Mama directing Daddy to do it another way. He wasn't making jokes and acting silly or complaining about what he was doing. He was simply caring for me in harmony with my mother.

And in that moment, there was a glimmer of hope that maybe my daddy really did love me after all. The way my mother did.

Show Boat

My mother had set up the ironing board in the middle of the den, and I could feel the heat of the iron from where I lay on the couch watching TV. The hissing steam mixed with the Niagara spray starch, creating a light, scented mist. My father sat in the recliner reading the newspaper and working the crossword puzzle.

I was watching the musical *Show Boat*. I was impressed, like almost everyone else, with the song that it's famous for, "Ol' Man River," and the amazing voice it took to sing that song. But a different song was far more powerful to me.

Most of the movie takes place on one of those big paddle boats that traveled up and down the Mississippi in the 1800s. The lead couple gets married, but then the husband leaves his wife before she has a chance to tell him that she's pregnant. His daughter spends the first five years of her life not knowing her father. Near the end of the movie he comes back and learns that he has a little girl, but she doesn't know who he is. They talk about playing make believe, then they sing the song, "Make Believe," a reprise of the one he sang as a duet with her mother at the beginning of the movie.

"Only make believe I love you,
Only make believe that you love me.
Others find peace of mind in pretending . . . "

I lay on the couch, with everything in me yearning for a father who adored me in the same way the man in the movie obviously adored his little girl.

As the father in the film poured out his love upon his little girl whom he didn't even know just because she was his, I could hardly choke back the tears. I wanted to crawl up on my father's lap and have him hold me while I cried. But I couldn't. After all, I reasoned, I was twelve and too old. But the honest truth was I had never felt free to do that. I could never let him see me cry. Sometimes he'd try to understand my tears, but more often than not he scoffed at them. The worst times were when they triggered anger.

Even if I had been brave enough to climb onto his lap, how would I explain what I was crying about? I hardly knew myself. Now I know that everything inside me grieved a relationship with a daddy I could trust. A daddy who was strong but gentle, able to teach me, to care for me, to be tender and playful. Here I was sitting in the same room with my father as I had night after night for twelve years, and felt the same emptiness I'd always felt, an emptiness that never went away—created by the absence of a father's love. I believed that not only did my daddy not love me—he didn't even like me.

The thing is, my father did love me. There were plenty of times that he paid attention to me and played with me. But a powerful distance kept me from knowing and experiencing that love. It was a distance he had created before I was old enough to realize it was there. There was also the distance I had created in order to stay safe. It was a distance that required help in navigating if I was expected to come closer to him.

It would be decades before we talked about that distance. Come to find out, he felt rejection from me. He thought that I didn't want to be close to him and that I preferred my mother.

Such a vicious cycle of pain and fear and rejection! Sadly, without anyone to help us wade through those murky waters of our own insecurities, we were unable to learn the truth until much later in life. But when we did get that help we were finally able to discover the truth—that this daddy loved his little girl, and the little girl wanted desperately to be close to her daddy.

That was when the healing began.

Two Men and a Boy

Ben was one of the men God put in my early life to show me men could be different from my father. When I was in elementary school, Ben and his friend Doug would frequently pop in, unannounced, to visit us in the evenings. They were in their twenties and were part of the singles group at church, a group my mom and dad had a special place in their heart for since they had been older singles. As a result, a collection of people who just didn't seem to fit in the broader fold of the church gravitated to my parents.

Ben was the oddity as the man who paid attention to me, who delighted in and appreciated my talents and personality, while Doug reinforced the norm as a man who didn't want to have much to do with me. Ben gave me a hug the minute he came through the door. Doug would walk right by me as though I wasn't there, saying absolutely nothing to me while warmly greeting my mom and dad.

Ben took a personal interest in me. He was a graphic designer and he did all the displays for McClurkan's department store. Sometimes we'd go by and visit him in the studio where he was coming up with new ideas for displays. He'd show me around and let me look at all of his art supplies. One time he helped me come up with an idea for the conservation poster contest for the fourth graders at my school. He helped me plan what to draw and we made up a slogan together.

Doug, on the other hand, was in the Air Force and had the personality of a wet mop. He was dry and sarcastic and got along really well with my parents.

Instead of realizing that the difference between Ben and Doug could be due to their personalities, I interpreted Doug's ignoring me as rejection—yet another man who didn't like me because there was something inadequate about this little girl that caused him to not want to interact. There weren't a lot of men who paid attention to me—and perhaps because of my dad's inconsistency in that area, I needed overt expressions of attention from men to realize that I could be valued by men for who I was.

My interpretation of Doug's disapproval heightened during the summer of 1973 when Ben came to visit Texas from Canada where he had moved after his wedding. Ben and his wife brought a boy along with them who lived alone with his mother and to whom Ben had become a father figure. Since Martin was only a year older than me, we spent every day playing together. That is, if he wasn't spending time with Doug.

Throughout the week Doug took Martin on outings, buying him a baseball cap, glove, bat, and ball. And he'd only known this kid a week. In contrast, he'd known me for a couple of years, coming to my house almost once a week, and he'd never given me a thing.

In my eleven-year-old mind I wondered why he had never paid the kind of attention to me that he had to Martin. As an adult I realize the truth could be any number of things, from Doug simply not knowing how, or feeling uncomfortable, or perhaps feeling it inappropriate for a man his age to pay attention to a young girl. As a child who hadn't had a lot of reassurance that she was worth a man's attention, this simply reinforced the lies I believed. Men pay more attention to you if you like things that boys like. If you do things that boys do. They like you more if you're a boy.

Why those lies grew deeper roots than the truths coming from men like Ben, who delighted in me for being the girl I most definitely was, I don't know.

The best thing about the summer of 1973, however, was that I developed my first crush on this Canadian boy named Martin. We played a lot of *Monopoly*, and sat in my tree house that was all of five feet off the ground. We played Putt-Putt. We played ping pong outside on our patio. Although my dad had taught me to play, it was Martin who drove me to be good. Good enough to win college intramurals ten years later. One day Martin and I played twenty-one games in a row and he beat me every time. For the first time in my life, I didn't care that I lost.

The day before he left to go back to Canada, my parents took us to the amusement park in town. We rode all the rides together, even the big Ferris wheel and the roller coaster, which I typically wouldn't ride with anyone but my dad. But I rode them with Martin. And loved it.

Afterward, as my parents were driving us to a party, Martin was leaning forward, hanging over the back of the front seat when he turned to look at me and asked, "Do you have a boyfriend?"

I was thrilled, but embarrassed that he was asking me in front of my parents. Sounding a lot like Gilda Radner's nerdy girl character on *Saturday Night Live*, I said, "Well, no."

He waited. And then he said, "What if I was your boyfriend?"

I grinned, shrugged my shoulders, and said, "Okay."

Ah, the simplicity of a define-the-relationship talk between an eleven-year-old girl and a twelve-year-old boy from two very different cultures. Somehow we managed to cross the divide. We never talked directly about it again, but for the next year and a half we wrote letters back and forth. He sent me presents for my birthday, at Christmas, and on Valentine's Day. I rationed the toffees that came from him at Christmas, making them last as long as I could, and the box of bubble bath beads he gave me for Valentine's day grew dusty because I didn't want to use them up.

The day after Martin left for home I told one of my friends on the phone how much I missed this boy and didn't know why. She just laughed at me.

Girl World

I had many friends throughout my life. The sad thing is, I didn't always know it. I thought the friendships were often one-sided. I thought no one wanted to be my friend as much as I wanted to be theirs. I was always looking for a place to belong, a place to fit in. Everywhere I looked, there didn't seem to be a puzzle piece shaped like Sally where she could fit.

Jennifer was my very first friend. She lived around the corner from me, and her house was the first place I ever got to walk to by myself, her phone number the first I learned to dial. With Jennifer I began learning what it felt like to be close to another female besides my mother, as well as be around someone who was my age. We played together a lot even though there were times when I had been terrified of her—like that time she left me up in the tree for one. Another time she coaxed me into the upstairs bathroom to look at something out the window. As I went to see what it was, she ran out the door and locked me in, telling me she was going to burn the house down. She struck something that sounded enough like a match to be believable— at least to a five-year-old. I was so afraid that I tried to open the window to escape. Jennifer stood on the other side of the door, laughing at me.

Then Lucy moved to town and she became friends with us, too. It was fun when we all played together, but there were times when they played at each other's houses without inviting me.

Then when we were together again, they had inside jokes I didn't know. They whispered secrets to each other in front of me, leaving me feeling left out. Sadly, as a result, I learned very early in life that, although you wanted friends to play with, you couldn't depend on them to stay the same, to always be your friend, no matter what. You couldn't depend on them to care for you or consider your feelings in the same way that you cared for theirs.

In the spring of my sixth-grade year, the strangest thing happened. I got to be friends with the country club girls. They were sort of like "the plastics" in the movie *Mean Girls*, only they weren't really mean, they just didn't associate with the other girls in our class. And I certainly didn't fit with them. Maybe it was because I wore my hair in braids every day, looking a bit like Pippi Longstocking. Or maybe because I liked to wear cowboy boots with the double knit pantsuits that had recently been deemed appropriate for girls to wear to school.

Toward the end of the year, a country club girl named Teresa sat in front of me in social studies. When we finished our work before the bell, she turned in her seat and talked to me. She seemed to be lonely. And she acted sincerely interested in learning about me and my life, my family, my church. She was an only child like me. Her parents were fighting a lot and considering a divorce. She had a bald patch starting on the side of her head, amidst a long flow of yellow-white hair that looked like silk when she flipped it past her shoulders. As much as she seemed to have a lot going for her, I felt sorry for her. Her story made me realize that, though my world wasn't perfect, I had much to be thankful for. Yet, how could it be possible that this country club girl would like to trade her life for mine?

During homeroom and lunch, Teresa invited me to sit with the other country club girls. So I sat at their table with my lunch I'd brought from home in my lunch box painted and shaped like Snoopy's doghouse, and waited for the rest of them to arrive with their cafeteria food. One of the girls said my lunches from home always looked better than anything the cafeteria was selling. I thought so, too.

To connect with these girls even more, I made up a board game that we played, chattering and giggling, during free time after lunch. The board game was a cross between *Life* and *Monopoly* that featured all of us and the things we did at school. For a while I thought my efforts at connecting were working, because that spring when I was eleven, wonder of wonders, Teresa invited me to her slumber party. I was beginning to think things were changing in the "girl world" for me.

I was excited. I was scared too because I wasn't completely secure in the whole spending-the-night-away-from-home thing. But I so wanted to go. My mother went all out and bought me a small tapestry overnight bag and a new pair of pajamas. I showed up right on time with my hair braided, wearing brown denim cut-off shorts, tennis shoes, and my dad's old sailor hat turned down. Teresa's mother was nice to me and showed me into the living room where I waited for the other girls to arrive. A lot of girls came. Girls I didn't know at all. Girls I knew only as acquaintances at school. The room was filled with girls, but there was no one I knew well enough to really talk to.

A bunch of boys came over later. We all trudged out to the patio, and most of the kids sat cross-legged in a circle with a Coke bottle in the middle. That was my first and only time to see a game of "Spin the Bottle." I stood off to the side with a handful of other girls who didn't play. I didn't want to play because

I didn't believe you were supposed to play games like that as a Christian. And I didn't play because I had no desire whatsoever to kiss a boy. To kiss anybody. Good grief, I was eleven.

I don't remember anything else we did that night. I don't remember talking to a soul the whole time I was there. I'm sure at some point Teresa must have acknowledged my presence; after all, it was her party.

I took my sleeping bag upstairs to the big playroom where we would all be sleeping and found a spot in the corner next to the TV where Wolfman Jack was hosting *The Midnight Special*. I watched the other girls traveling in packs and pairs, giggling, bumping into me as they were playing with each other, and glancing at me with an, "Oh, sorry." I wanted so badly to be a part of them, to feel like I fit with them, but I just didn't. I didn't hide out; I had been taught better than that. I went ahead and acted as if I was supposed to be there and as though I was having as grand a time as everyone else.

Later I went into the bathroom and changed into my pajamas, pajamas like no one else had on, crawled into my sleeping bag, and in the midst of whispered conversations in the dark, and bursts of laughter from girls still awake downstairs, I curled up with the TV and let Helen Reddy's "I Am Woman" lull me to sleep.

That night serves in my memory as a metaphor for how I've felt all my life about being a girl. I was in a sea of girls, and although nobody was overtly hateful to me, no one pointed at me and laughed or called me names, I knew I didn't belong. I acted as though I did, but inside I knew I was all alone.

In the fifth grade I became close friends with a girl named Allison. We both loved music and reading and didn't care to play outside.

We played together at recess and did everything we possibly could together.

Allison and I sat right across from each other in spelling class. During the weekly spelling test we had a race to see who could spell the word the fastest and put our pens down first. It was usually a tie because Allison and I were of comparable ability.

That spring we were in the middle of our spelling test with our teacher, Miss Berry, calling the words out to us, slowly repeating the word a second and third time. Allison and I finished the word after hearing it the first time and often grinned or giggled at each other because we got it so quickly. But on that day, after one of the words was called, I never saw Allison look up. She never put her pen down. It fell out of her hand and clattered to the floor beside her desk because her hand was shaking so badly. I looked over at her and her whole body was shaking so violently that she fell to the floor.

Allison writhed on the floor, her eyes rolling back in her head. Miss Berry called for someone to get the teacher next door, while at the same time tearing a piece of her slip and wrapping the cloth around a pen. She bent over my friend and opened her mouth to put the pen in to hold down her tongue.

I was terrified, not understanding what was happening, but feeling safe, certain Miss Berry knew exactly what to do.

Our reading teacher from across the hall took the class to the library where we all sat at the tables and waited. The kids in my class started talking about what had happened and what was going to happen to Allison. Some of them said she was going to die. Some said she was already dead. I wanted them all to shut up. They weren't doctors; they didn't know. I didn't know what was wrong with her, but I didn't want the rest of the kids to say she wasn't going to be okay. What would I do if she wasn't?

We later found out that Allison had had a seizure—her first—and that it would take her awhile to recover, but that she would eventually come back to school. I was thrilled when she came back. I didn't notice it at first, but over time I realized there was something different about her. The obvious difference was that she was slower on the spelling tests. I went to school every day expecting to be with my friend, Allison, and yet someone else now occupied her body. She was similar, but she wasn't the Allison I knew. Seeing her like that made me feel as if I had lost another friend.

We were both selected to play the role of Mary in the PTA Christmas pageant that year. Allison got to be the Mary who rode the papier-mâché donkey we all helped make in art class, and I had to be the Mary who sat in the stable with Robert, the boy who played Joseph. Our role required us to stare at a doll who was supposed to be the baby Jesus lying in a bed of hay.

I was embarrassed playing Mary, a woman who'd just had a baby. It gave me the creeps. I also felt uncomfortable sitting there with this boy who was supposed to be playing my husband. Whenever I played house with my friends, which wasn't too often because I didn't particularly care for playing house, I was always the husband. The father. And now here I was sitting in front of all these people in the Ben Franklin Elementary School cafeteria playing the mother of all mothers. I loved the fact that my music teacher had picked me, and I agreed to do it because of her and because it was an honor to play the role of Jesus' mother. But no one—no one but Jesus himself—knew how miserable it was for me to play that part. I had no idea why it bothered me so much. I wished that if I had to be Mary at all they would have let me be Allison's Mary.

I'M A GIRL!

Right before I started seventh grade, I cut my hair. I had beautiful long, dirty blond hair that was clear down to my rear. I'd worn it in braids most of the time during sixth grade, my mother braiding my hair every morning before school. When I left it down, it was really pretty. But I didn't like messing with my hair and I didn't want to keep wearing braids. After all, I was in the seventh grade.

The real reason I cut my hair, but didn't admit to myself, was that I wanted to look like Julie Andrews. *The Sound of Music* made a comeback that summer and I went to see it every afternoon the week it was showing at the State Theater downtown. I loved Julie Andrews. I wanted to be Julie Andrews. And Julie Andrews had short hair playing Maria Von Trapp. She was strong and extremely feminine at the same time. She was precisely what I wanted to be.

So I cut all my hair off. The haircut was cute and it looked just like Julie Andrews' hair. But I was twelve, a late bloomer who didn't know anything about curling irons, hot rollers, or a blow dryer. My mother was no help. She was born in 1921 and people from that era did well to wash their hair once a week. In her mind, a good set of brush rollers, bobby pins, a rat-tail comb, and a large supply of heavy duty hairspray are all you need to keep your hair looking good. Bless her heart, she had no idea what to do with my hair. Her classic comment was, "Oh, honey, why are you washing your hair? You just washed it three days ago." And how many times did I hear the lecture on how I was going to catch cold with a wet head? Since Mama wouldn't let me go outside with a wet head, if I didn't get up in time to wash and dry my hair, I couldn't wash it at all. That meant most mornings I went to school with a greasy mess of hair.

In an effort to save money, my mother started making clothes for me and sixth grade was the year that she found the pinafore pattern. I had pinafores of every color and design—some to wear as dresses, some to wear as smocks. When it got cooler, I wore the pinafore over a long sleeved shirt. I wasn't fat, but I thought I was. I was chunky. So between my short, greasy hair, my gold-rimmed glasses, and my chunky little body wearing pinafores over bell bottom pants and tennis shoes, I was a sight to behold.

On the inside I was a little girl with a heart of gold, but given my shapeless body, my haircut made me look like a boy. That possibility had never entered my mind when I cut all my hair off, and it really hurt my feelings when people mistook me for a boy. It got so bad that when it became popular for girls to wear chambray work shirts embroidered with different designs, I had my mother embroider the phrase "I Am a Girl!" on the back of my shirt. Of course, no one thought to tell me that if you put that on a shirt it would only make the situation worse. Kids and adults alike ribbed me, "Yeah, you have to tell people you're a girl, 'cause nobody can tell!"

I had just turned thirteen in the fall of my eighth-grade year when my family went to the Piccadilly cafeteria downtown after church. I thought I looked especially sharp that morning in my new pin-stripe denim skirt that fell just above my knees and a maroon sweater vest over a cream-colored long-sleeved shirt. I wore knee socks with high-heeled denim saddle-oxfords. I'd even washed my hair that morning so it looked cute. I'm telling you, I was the look of 1974 that morning. We pushed our trays along the cafeteria line and I stopped in front of the lady standing behind the counter serving rolls. She looked up at me, tongs in hand, smiled warmly, and said, "Bread, sir?"

I thought for certain she should've seen me coming down the serving line, my skirt a big clue to my sex, but maybe she wasn't paying attention. I was humiliated. I wanted the floor to open up and swallow me. I thought that if I still didn't look like a girl even while wearing a dress, then there must be nothing about me that looked like a girl. I was embarrassed and tired of feeling embarrassed. I wanted to grab those tongs out of her fat hand and beat her with them.

I started to scream on the inside. "Can't you people see that I'm a girl? Seriously, what do I have to do?"

A part of me was furious, fighting to be the girl I believed I was supposed to be. I didn't feel like I was any good at being a girl, and eventually I believed I didn't have what it took to be a girl. Another part of me believed that it would have been better for me to be a boy and to stop fighting it. The voice inside my head grew louder. You talk like a boy, you look like a boy. There's a reason nobody tells you you're pretty. They don't even think you're a girl—they think you're a boy. Even in a dress.

When anybody told me how much I looked like my dad, I wanted to hit them. Partly because I didn't want to look like him, but more so because I thought girls were supposed to look like their mothers. Only boys were supposed to look like their dads.

It didn't help that a friend of my mother's always went on and on about how she could pick me out of a two-hundred-piece band marching on the football field because I walked like my dad. Everybody laughed and thought that was so funny. I never thought it was funny. Girls were supposed to walk differently than boys. I heard men watched the way women walked, and that was a part of what attracted men to women. But they obviously wouldn't be watching me because I walked like my dad, which meant I walked like a man.

Seventh Grade

Seventh grade meant starting junior high, and we were required to attend a day of orientation so we would know our way around the school. In seventh grade you were on your own, and you got to choose elective subjects in addition to the basic subjects that everyone took, like math, history, science and English. And P.E. Everyone had to take P.E. Every day.

My mom drove me and we walked into the big auditorium at the junior high that was already packed full of kids. Kids who had traveled there in packs or at least in pairs, whose mothers had dropped them off and left. A few of the mothers stayed. But not many. My mother did, sitting with me at the very back of the auditorium. As I glanced around to see if I saw any of my friends from elementary school, I noticed that the country club girls were sitting front and center of the auditorium.

For a number of reasons I didn't have much contact with other kids over the summer, so I felt like someone who had been in the desert for three months, dying of thirst, and then spotted water. Conveniently minimizing my encounter with these girls at the slumber party the previous spring and how little they had interacted with me then, I told my mom I was going to sit with my friends and bounded out of my seat toward the front of the auditorium.

I couldn't wait to see these girls, and it never entered my mind that they might not feel the same about me. When I got to their row, I stood in the aisle and slowly the whole row turned and looked at me as I said, "Hi!" The girls glanced at me and mumbled an unenthusiastic, "Hi" back, quickly returning to their conversations amongst themselves. The girl on the end was left in the awkward situation of having to make conversation with me since I was standing there in the aisle, but it didn't take long for me to get the hint. I said goodbye to them, as though it had never been my intention to stay and sit with them.

Here I was, standing in front of an auditorium packed full of my peers, unsure of myself in starting this new chapter of my life, facing the long walk up the aisle, all the way to the rear of the auditorium to sit with my mother. It was humiliating. But I walked with my head up and smiled as though I was doing exactly what I wanted, and that it didn't bother me at all to be seen sitting with my mother.

I settled in my seat knowing that as long as I could keep to myself that I didn't fit, it wasn't as painful. When the whole world recognizes that you don't fit, that you're not wanted by this group you want to be a part of, well, that feels even worse.

Laurie moved to town when I was in the seventh grade and she became the closest friend I'd ever had. Almost a foot taller than me, she had long dark hair, twinkly blue eyes, and an olive complexion. Laurie was the girl that everyone knew when she got past the awkward middle school stage she was going to be a knock-out. There was a perpetual smile on her face and a giggle about to happen.

Laurie was the friend I shared secrets with and whispered things to, even though you knew at the age of twelve that whispering was rude. Laurie was the friend I talked to on the phone at night, even though I'd talked to her all day at school. She was the friend I stayed overnight with, taking turns at each other's houses on the weekends.

More than any other person in my life, I felt free to talk about boys with Laurie. We watched the boys in choir and we talked about the ones in band. We giggled about them. Although Laurie had a new crush every week, there was one boy in particular for me. She knew I liked Kenneth, and for once in my life I wasn't embarrassed about liking someone. She's the one who didn't seem awkward as she explained to me what French kissing was, and I wondered what that would feel like with Kenneth. And I didn't feel awkward admitting to her that I couldn't stand that he hadn't asked me to the eighth-grade band banquet.

And my mother liked Laurie.

Laurie was the only friend I had that I felt as if I could be close to without upsetting my mother. Every other friend, at some point, had fallen out of favor with my mom, and it forever changed the tone of our relationship.

It was obvious to me when my mother didn't like one of my friends. Her sweet tone that made everybody around her feel loved and comfortable turned to a cold distance. Her responses became subtle verbal and nonverbal cues sent through her tone of voice or facial expression. These changes in her mannerisms were so slight that most people wouldn't even realize what was happening, but I always knew.

I always felt nervous when my mom and a friend were together, knowing at some point my mother would probably find something she didn't like. Not enough to dismiss the friendship, but a disapproval transmitted in a sort of code. A code that I'd had to learn to understand since I was very little because my very survival depended on pleasing my mom.

The dislike could be the result of the friend hurting my feelings and my mother's overprotection kicking in. Rather than simply letting us work it out, she held that action against her. Or she found some trait of the girl's that she didn't like and overreacted, wanting me to find fault with her, too.

I interpreted her messages to say that she didn't want me to spend time with this person, let alone be close to her. Once I became close to someone, especially a girl, I always felt that unspoken, unacknowledged tension. And then I felt trapped between having to choose my friend or my mother. It worsened as I got older, and in order to keep from constantly feeling on edge, I learned to keep my friends at a distance.

I don't believe my mother intentionally sabotaged my friendships or that she was even aware of the effect of her actions. I believe she had good intentions in seeking out the best relationships for me. But the sad thing is that perhaps underneath was a desire to keep me close. It added to the unconscious belief that I really couldn't trust people, nor could I be close to anyone but her.

Even though Laurie was the only close friend with whom I didn't feel that sense of competition between she and my mom, by the time I was twelve, I doubted anyone wanted to be "best friends" with me anyway. I didn't believe someone would desire being close to me as much as I desired being close to them. For whatever reason, I never felt that I had that best friend. The sad thing is, I did. I just couldn't see it.

Gym Class

If religion had been emphasized in my household growing up to the same degree that physical exercise was encouraged, I would be an atheist today.

Having older parents meant we didn't do much of anything that might induce a sweat. So by the time I was twelve I hadn't developed any athletic skills and I despised the idea of having to take P.E. I was well aware that movement and coordination weren't things I excelled in, and nobody was happier than I was when it rained and we had indoor recess. But the things we were expected to do in seventh grade P.E. took my humiliation to a whole new level.

Junior high P.E. meant having to change your clothes in a locker room with a bunch of other girls and then taking a shower in the middle of the day. At school.

Our class had about forty girls. We were divided into squads with an eighth-grade girl as our squad leader. I was "lucky" to have Rhonda as my squad leader. Rhonda was void of any compassion for an uncoordinated, nerdy white girl. Completely opposite me, she excelled in athletics, not in academics. Every day Rhonda made my life a living hell in gym class. She laughed at me. Not only did she laugh at me, but she hollered for all her friends to come observe yet another feat of athletic prowess that I hadn't mastered.

"Hey, all y'all, come over here and look at dis girl. She cain't do nuthin'! Watch her try ta do a sit-up. See? Girl, I cain't believe you dat bad. Cain't chu do nuthin'?"

Everyone gathered around me while I demonstrated that I couldn't do a sit-up or a handstand. I wouldn't even give them the pleasure of seeing me attempt a cartwheel. Rhonda's friends laughed hysterically along with her, but the other girls just stood there. Some grinned, perhaps out of embarrassment, knowing that what Rhonda was doing wasn't very nice, but they didn't do anything to stop her either.

The gym teacher, Coach Thompson, didn't do anything--she was in her office smoking cigarettes. Some days Coach Thompson would emerge from her smoke-filled room in gray sweats to watch my failures along with the rest of the class. Never once did the teacher offer to help me. Never once did she make Rhonda stop calling attention to me. And nobody ever said "Atta girl!" when, after not being able to do a single sit-up at the first of the semester, I could do ten by the end.

The six weeks we learned gymnastics, the gym was filled with uneven parallel bars, a pommel horse, and rings. Mats spread over almost every inch of the gym floor. Girls were running and jumping and swinging and catapulting themselves off the walls. Meanwhile, I couldn't even turn a somersault.

At home, both my parents, now in their fifties, got down on the kitchen floor to help me learn to turn a somersault. I never quite got the hang of it, but at least I could do enough to pass Rhonda's inspection.

Every day I tried to be gymnastic. Every day I ran toward that pommel horse with all the gusto I had, hoping to channel just enough of Nadia Comăneci to make it over, but each time I stopped dead in my tracks when I reached it.

Years later when I had found what I could do well—public speaking—I tried to remember what that repeated failure had felt like. So no matter how hard it was for kids to get through speeches in my class, I found some way to encourage them.

The worst six weeks of gym class, though, was without a doubt basketball. At that time, I'd never seen girls play basketball, only boys. And I'd been to a lot of boys' basketball games. So there I was in the classic scene where two captains are choosing their teams. It comes down to the end and the only ones left are all the fat kids and the ones who still don't know they aren't supposed to pick their noses in front of people. And me. I hated being the last one picked so much that I worked really hard on developing enough mannerisms to make myself look athletic. That way, if the captain didn't really know me, and hadn't seen me play a sport, she wouldn't know I wasn't any good.

Coach Thompson made sure that all of us got picked at least once during the six weeks so that everyone got a chance to play in one game. No one was more excited about that than me. None of them knew I was actually quite good at dribbling a basketball. At home I'd go outside and bounce a basketball on the patio. I didn't have a hoop, so I didn't learn to shoot, but at least I could dribble.

When I got in the game, I was thrilled when somebody overthrew the ball and I actually kept it from going out of bounds. I think everyone was shocked, so we all froze for a second in amazement, and then I realized I had to do something. I was already near the half-court line. I dribbled like a pro, running toward the goal ahead of me. I reached it and shot the ball. Like a scene from *Hoosiers*, it swooped through the net, seemingly in slow motion. I was ecstatic. I jumped up and down in complete and utter joy—until I looked around to see a mob of angry girls coming toward me, the opposing team shrieking in delight, and the rest of the girls from my class sitting in the stands laughing.

Not remembering the half court rules, I had crossed the line and made a goal for the other team.

III
The Lies Grow Deeper

Fifteen

My sophomore year in high school was clearly one of the worst years of my life.

If people are honest, I'm not sure anyone would say they enjoyed their sophomore year of high school. A lot of things happen in that year of adolescence—big things, but little things, too. Things that appear insignificant at the time, but you look back on them later and realize they were huge. Things that you don't quite know what to do with when you're fifteen. Things that nobody really wants to talk about. At least they didn't in 1976.

That year I had big things to worry about. For starters, I was desperately trying to figure out whether to cut my hair again or let it grow out. I had been trying to let it grow because I thought it looked horrible most of the time. And the truth is, it did. In 1976 there were only so many ways girls wore their hair—you either had Farrah Fawcett hair, Dorothy Hamill hair, or Marcia Brady hair. My hair didn't fit into any of those categories, and, like most girls, I was so self-focused I didn't realize my friends' hair didn't either.

I had another good reason to want my hair to grow out. Maybe then people would stop thinking I looked like a boy. But I didn't know how to fix it while it was growing out, and I got tired of waiting for it to look okay. So I cut it all off again. That made matters worse.

I also spent too much time wondering when I would have a waist and when I would need to wear anything beyond a training bra. I was wondering if and when anything even remotely close to what my friends and I read out of *Ode to Billy Joe* late one night at a slumber party would ever happen to me. All of my friends and I huddled around Lucy while she read a scene to us out loud about a boy and girl on a blanket in the grass. As she read, I wondered what that would be like. And I wondered whom I identified with most in the scene—the boy or the girl. Because at fifteen I was very confused about who I was supposed to be.

As much as I wanted to be a girl, by the time I was fifteen being a girl was not only scary to me, everything about it was extremely embarrassing. Some of the clothes you had to wear were embarrassing—especially the underwear. I hated the word "panties" and refused to say it. When you first started to wear a bra, boys walked by your desk at school and popped the strap and laughed.

The most horrifying part of being a girl, though, was having a period. Or at least that's what I took away from "the talk" my mother had with me in the fifth grade. This particular talk didn't include anything about sex—that talk came three years later, in the car on the way home from school. That conversation was all of ten minutes. And that was the only conversation we ever had about sex.

As limited as both of those conversations were, I'm thankful my mother at least made an attempt to talk to me, because I've met lots of women whose mothers never explained a thing to them about sex, or even about their menstrual cycle.

"The talk" about having a period came after they showed these films at school—one for girls and one for boys—called *Our Growing Bodies*. My mom didn't sign the release form for me to watch it, so I was the only girl in the entire fifth grade who didn't see the film. Instead, I sat in the library for an hour with the librarian. I was fine with that except that everyone looked at me with an, "Oh, you poor thing, I wonder what's wrong with you that you can't watch this?" expression on their faces as they filed out of class. I then understood how Jehovah's Witness kids must have felt when they had to leave the classroom during the pledge of allegiance or during Halloween and Christmas parties.

When the film was over, the girls filed back into class, giggling because they knew something I didn't. They were now part of a special sorority and knew the secret handshake and I didn't. They asked me why I didn't see the film, and I told them my mother didn't want me to see it until she could talk to me. Then they giggled more.

My mother was one of those women whose mother had never talked to her about anything. She had to learn about having a period and anything sexual on her own, so she didn't want that for me. But I think it must've been a talk she dreaded. On the same day they showed the film, when I got home from school, we went back into the den and her nervousness hung in the room, as though what she wanted to say was going to be the worst news ever. I felt this ominous sense of dread. The den was dark to begin with, but on that day it was the bottom of Carlsbad Cavern at the end of the tour when they turn off all the lights.

She told me about what happened once a month, and based on what she said, there was nothing good about it. Having a period made you feel bad. It was a part of "the curse of Eve." Everything she said made being a girl even less appealing and more difficult. Another thing to be embarrassed about. Another thing to prove that being a girl was a lot of trouble.

At the time I didn't realize that you didn't have to feel that way about being a girl and I thought everyone felt that way. After all, even my mother was embarrassed.

Men seemed embarrassed or reluctant to talk about anything related to being a girl as well. Between silence from men, crude jokes from boys in class, and characters like Archie Bunker on TV saying things like, "I don't want to hear nothin' about the female ailments," I was ashamed of being female.

Although being a girl was a constant source of embarrassment, there were things about being a girl that I really enjoyed. I could spend hours walking around the mall looking at clothes and purses and shoes. I loved *Seventeen* magazine and didn't go anywhere without my Bonnie Bell lip smacker. I loved music and literature and John Boy Walton. In my understanding, all those things made you a girl, but having a period *really* made you a girl. My mom told me it was something you couldn't escape, but somehow I did. At least for a while.

By the time I was fifteen, I may have had only one or two periods. Then, all through high school and college my menstrual cycle was spasmodic at best. I went for months at a time without having a regular period. Since my mom had started her cycle when she was twelve, she thought my situation was some sort of blessing instead of considering the possibility that something might be wrong. It wasn't problematic to me either. In fact, I liked it just fine. One less trouble associated with being a girl. But I desperately wanted to be one of the girls.

I wanted to look a little more like them. My body just wasn't changing like other girls' bodies. I'm not only talking about moving out of the training bra. I'm talking about the whole package. I felt awkward and chunky, and didn't quite know what to do with myself just like a lot of fifteen-year-old girls—whether they've developed yet or not. But when your body doesn't look like other girls' bodies—at least to the degree that other kids think that it should—well, you know what happens.

That year I asked Kenneth to be my date for the annual band banquet that would be held in the Country Club ballroom—the most elegant place in town, and one of the few places large enough to accommodate three or four hundred people.

The boys wore double-knit suits with wide lapels or leisure suits with obnoxious white piping and huge gaudy ties. The girls wore slinky jersey knit dresses with spaghetti straps or simple peasant dresses. Kenneth went with a traditional, conservative suit and tie, and I went with the peasant look. We rode with our friend, Russell, and his date because Russell was the only one of us who already had his driver's license. As we stepped into the ballroom, I thought we were one of the cutest couples there.

It was a wonderful night. I enjoyed being a girl all dressed up on a date with a boy. A boy I really liked. A boy who was funny and sweet and smart. A boy I hoped would like me and be proud of being with me. I sat at a table full of our friends who had come as couples to this big, end-of-the-year celebration and felt happy. Completely content. Until we came to the "Wills and Prophecies" portion of the program.

The seniors had a tradition of making bequests to the under-classmen in a "last will and testament." They made certain pre-dictions about the future of the band and its members. Most of the time they were funny and occasionally they were sweet. But sometimes they said things that cut deeply. Maybe because they were just kids themselves, they didn't know how deep.

Her name was Cathy, and she played the saxophone. Tall and slender with long, shiny light brown hair, Cathy was one of those girls who looked like she had it all together—even if she was in the band. She was a senior and I was a sophomore, so we didn't know each other very well. In fact, I don't think we'd ever actually spoken to one another. But in the prophecies that year at the banquet, Cathy spoke of me.

"To Sally Gary I leave a membership at the gym . . . so she can get a figure."

It was one of those moments in a TV sitcom where the sound becomes garbled and the main character shrinks down to a miniature version of herself while everyone laughs hysterically. It was a nightmare. All I heard from every direction was laughter. The fact that everybody laughed confirmed that they had been thinking the same thing. They had just never said it out loud. I looked around at my friends at our table and even they were laughing. I looked at Kenneth and thank goodness, he wasn't laughing. I leaned over and asked him if they were trying to say I was fat, and he said, "No, no, you're not fat. She just means you don't have any boobs."

Thanks, Kenneth.

My mom had always taught me to laugh at myself, so that nobody could truly be laughing at me. So I laughed that night and pretended the prophecy didn't bother me. But on the inside, the girl in me was crushed.

Singing

It was also in my sophomore year of high school that I found out I couldn't sing.

The 1970s marked the rise of the musical variety show on TV, and it seemed as if everybody who was anybody was singing. All of the women I wanted to be like could sing. Even Mary Tyler Moore did musicals. With Julie Andrews, no less.

Singing also seemed to be something all the women in my world did—the women at church, my mother's friends, the women in my family. Singing a cappella harmony was a part of our Church of Christ tradition. Any time we had a gathering at church, we sang. When we went to people's homes or when they came to ours, we often sang. My grandmother sang, warbly and a bit off-key, but she still sang. My mother had a beautiful, strong alto voice. When we were at home, she played the piano and sang, her voice booming over the keys. Driving around town, she sang.

I kept believing that when I grew up, just because I was a woman, I'd be able to sing like my mother.

By the sixth grade, just like her, I could sing the alto part at church. But somewhere in the beginning of middle school I noticed the lower voice harmonies in church—the men's voices. One man sang the tenor line so loudly that you could hear him no matter where he sat. I began paying attention to that harmony and soon realized I could sing tenor, too. I had more control over my voice in that range and it sounded stronger than when I tried to sing alto. I liked that a girl singing tenor was different, unique. I kept reminding myself that Karen Carpenter had a lower voice range, and was a girl drummer. You just didn't get any cooler than that.

My high school had a prestigious choir known as A Cappella. Even though the choir members wore robes and had to learn classical music, it was so prestigious that even some football players wanted to be a part of it. Only juniors and seniors could be in A Cappella. With rare exception the director took students who hadn't been singing in the girls' or mixed choirs as freshmen and sophomores.

Since singing was something I was supposed to be able to do as a female member of my family, and as a member of the Church of Christ, even though I wasn't in either one of the beginning choirs, I was brazen enough to go ahead and try out.

I don't remember what I sang. I don't remember if I brought my own piece or if the director had one that he had everyone sing. What I remember most though is the expression on his face when he realized I could hit a "D" below middle "C." And then out of sheer curiosity he started playing notes down the scale, a half step at a time.

"Do you think you could hit this?" he'd ask me. Then he'd play the note.

"And this?"

I made it down to a "B" flat below "C" below middle "C" before I could go no further without growling. He stared at me in amazement, and I left the audition that morning not knowing whether it was a good thing or a bad thing. Monday when he posted the list and my name wasn't on it, I was crushed. But I didn't give up.

Later that year I agreed to sing a duet with one of our family friends at a church talent show. Paul and I decided to sing "Luckenbach, Texas," like Waylon Jennings and Willie Nelson. *The Gong Show* was popular on TV at that time, so the church decided to have our own version, with judges who "gonged" acts if they didn't like them. I was scared to death. I'd never sung a solo before, and I had to sing the whole opening by myself.

"The only two things in life that make it worth livin' –
is guitars that tune good . . ."

I pitched it almost as low as Waylon sang it himself—and then Paul came in for the chorus and I switched over to harmony.

"Let's go to Luckenbach, Texas, with Willy and Waylon and the boys."

We'd barely gotten to the second line when the gong sounded and the audience erupted in laughter. Paul played it up with total indignation and egged the audience on to laugh more.

What the audience, the judges, and even Paul didn't know was how devastating that was to a teenaged girl who already doubted her ability to sing—and who tied the ability to sing with something that you were supposed to be able to do if you were a woman. I had doubted my ability to sing before, and being "gonged" by people at church clinched it.

On the outside, I laughed it off. No one ever knew how crushed I was on the inside. I found out later that the judges were Paul's friends and they were playing a joke on him. Sadly, none of those adults ever stopped to think of the effect that might have on a fifteen-year-old girl. Or maybe they saw a girl who looked confident, who could take a joke, and never thought their joke would bother her. And as most narcissistic teenagers might, I thought the reason they gonged us was because I couldn't sing.

"Son"

Looking back at pictures of me from high school, I was never fat. But I always believed I was. My body didn't look like the pictures of girls my age in *Seventeen* magazine; you know, the way you're supposed to look. I was gangly with long arms and skinny legs, a belly and no waist. I looked a lot like those pictures in *National Geographic* of starving children in Africa, ribs sticking out above distended stomachs and toothpick limbs. Well, I didn't really look like that. But I sure felt like I did.

As a sophomore I decided to cut my hair again, but instead of looking like Dorothy Hamill, I looked more like John Boy Walton—and a part of me liked it that way.

I wore glasses because the only contact lenses available at the time were hard ones, and the thought of putting something like that in my eyes gave me the creeps. The most popular frames for glasses that year were tortoise shell aviators, so that's what I picked out. I wore jeans and T-shirts and tennis shoes, and for the most part I think I looked like everybody else, but still, there was something different about me.

When I was in high school I never heard anybody being made fun of for being homosexual, except for my friend, Coy Stith, and that was mostly because he wore clogs and was rather loud and obnoxious. But it wasn't something you accused some-one of unless you were absolutely certain. No one ever accused me or made fun of me for being homosexual. But every day of my sophomore year in health class three boys called me "Son."

Bobby sat behind me and Tiger and Mike sat across the row from me. When they tired of having any substantive conversation between themselves—which took all of five minutes—they turned to making fun of me.

"Hey, Son, do you know you look like a boy?"

"Are you sure you're a girl?"

"Doesn't she look like a boy?"

"Yeah, she looks more like a boy than she does a girl."

"Man, what's the matter with you—you supposed to be a boy?"

"Hey, Son, how you doin' today?"

"Did you shave this morning, Son?"

Every single day they harassed me, like they were talking to a younger boy that they were trying to teach the ropes in every area of life, equipping me to be a "real man." If I responded with silence, I heard, "Now, Son, don't get upset . . . . Oh, Son, we've hurt your feelings, we're so sorry . . . ." If I tried to go along with them or tease them back, it made it worse. No matter how I reacted, the harassment never stopped.

Our uninvolved teacher was one of the assistant football coaches. During class he had us working on questions from our textbooks or watching a film while he sat at his desk and read the newspaper.

What fifteen-year-old girl wants to go up to the coach/ teacher who looks like he could double for Superman and ask him to please make the three athletes stop calling her "Son?"

Every day during my sophomore year those messages were pumped into me. "You're more like a boy, Sally. Everyone thinks it, everybody knows it—it's just that these three guys actually say it out loud." Although not overt, the messages played like a soft, continuous, subtle undercurrent in my head creating a fog through which I saw myself. I look like a boy. I sing like a boy.

It seemed to me that if I really was pretty, someone would have told me by the time I was fifteen. But no one had—besides my mother. She'd turn to my father and say, "Doesn't she look pretty, Dan?" He'd glance up from the newspaper and say, "Yeah," then go right back to his reading.

Voices within urged me to keep trying to find myself, to figure out how to do this girl thing. But the more awkward I felt around the other girls, the less I sought them out. And the less I sought them out, the fewer opportunities I had to learn from them. Even I knew there was only so much I could learn from watching *The Mary Tyler Moore Show* and reading *Seventeen*.

But I thought I should know the basics of being a girl by now. It was like being too embarrassed to learn to swim or ride a bike after a certain age.

So I kept on trying to be the best girl I knew how to be. And I prayed that as I grew up something would just happen to fix it. Maybe that was what growing up was all about. One morning I would wake up and suddenly know what I was supposed to know about being a woman.

Maybe I would also look like Farrah Fawcett and sing like Karen Carpenter.

Stranger Among Us

I came home from school one day to find my mother terribly upset. When she was upset about something, she pretended she wanted to keep it from me, as though she were protecting me. But it was written all over her face that she did, in fact, want to tell me about it.

This day reminded me of the time when I was eleven years old and I went with her to a doctor's appointment. The moment she came to get me from the waiting room, I knew something was wrong. I could read it in her face, her expressions, her tone of voice. I had spent so much of my life becoming keenly aware of the slightest variation in her mannerisms. It was like I had an intuitive built-in radar on high alert tuned to my mother's feelings. My mother was all I had to count on—she was my stability, my savior, my everything.

On that day there was no question in my mind that something was up. As we waited in the drugstore for a prescription to be filled, she let me get ice cream at the fountain. From that vantage point I noticed her whispers to the pharmacist's wife and close friend from church, Wanda. I watched my mother's face. I watched Wanda's face. I saw Wanda touch my mother's arm. The hand holding and squeezing before letting go. The pat, pat, pat of Wanda's hand on my mother's before rejoining the drugstore world. Bad news had been exchanged and I knew it. So I badgered my mother until she told me about the grapefruit-sized tumor she needed to have surgically removed. As soon as possible. Before I finished the sixth grade.

Seeing my mother sitting on the couch that day in the spring of my sophomore year felt very much like that moment in the drugstore, and I wondered what had my mom so upset. Another tumor? More surgery? Did somebody die?

She asked me to come sit beside her on the sofa. Unfortunately, this time she spared no detail in telling me what had happened. Whether it was out of shock or fear, or simply not knowing what to do, she told me everything. I wished she hadn't.

I realized she was frightened. She stuttered, like she did in those times she sensed my father might become violent—in those times she stood up to him to defend me by positioning herself between us. Her body might appear calm, but her voice told me she was scared. Really scared.

She told me about a phone call she had received earlier that afternoon from a man. She recalled every detail about the conversation, telling me that the man obviously knew us because he referenced things that only someone who was well acquainted with us would know. He called my mother by name. He knew my dad's name. He knew my name. He knew where we lived. Where we sat in church on Sunday mornings. He knew I was in the high school Sunday school class. He knew that my mother was the coordinator for the primary grade Sunday school classes, and he knew that my father served as a deacon. He knew what my mother had worn to church the Sunday before. After he established that he knew all those things about us through seemingly friendly conversation, he quizzed my mom to discover if she knew who she was talking to. "Are you sure you don't know who this is?" he asked. He casually asked her if she was home alone. And then he asked her if she'd like for him to come over and rape her.

Those words stung me then, and they sting today as I write them. She told me the rest of the things he said, I think more out of shock than anything else. Because she was frightened and I was her confidante. I wished she hadn't told me what he would do to her and to me if she ever told.

My mom kept him on the line, straining to identify the voice and eventually she did. My parents were friends with many of the younger couples who were actively involved at church, and he was in that group. He and his wife hadn't lived there very long and I don't think they stayed very long after that.

I wanted to bash his head in with a baseball bat. He had threatened my mother. He had threatened me. Didn't he know we'd already been scared enough? We didn't need any more. I wanted to glare at him from the moment I walked into my Sunday school classroom where he was a volunteer until the bell signaled it was time to leave. I wanted to scream and out him for the cowardly fiend he was. How dare all the other men stand around and laugh and talk with him after what he'd done! Didn't they know? Couldn't anyone see that during the week he wasn't who he claimed to be on Sunday morning?

I swallowed it all and never let my feelings show. No one ever knew how frightened I was. Or how angry I was. Or how powerless I felt as a girl.

To my knowledge, nothing was ever said or done. I continued to go to class and participate and be actively involved in the youth group. But any time that man was around, I was afraid.

In the fifth grade, a classmate had asked me if I knew what "rape" meant. When I said I didn't, she proceeded to tell me that rape was what a man did to a girl, explaining that he did that "because he was mad at her."

I never told anyone, not even my mother, but from then on I was petrified that when my father was mad at me or my mother, he might do that awful thing to us. When he was angry and not talking to us in the house, I slept with an antique glass whiskey bottle I'd gotten on vacation in Colorado tucked underneath my pillow. Just in case. Because you never knew. You never knew what a man might do if he got angry enough.

And now this guy affirmed that men were scary and unpredictable. Even at church. Like the men in my family. It drove the message home that there's not a lot you can do to stand up for yourself if you're a girl, and that even the good men don't always know how to protect you. Men definitely had it better than women because they couldn't be threatened like women. They were stronger physically and could protect themselves more easily.

I wanted to believe that somewhere there might be men who were safe. Who were kind and predictable. Who would love me for me. Who wouldn't mind that I was smart. And funny. Someone who would know that underneath all the outgoing façade was a very introverted girl—tenderhearted, compassionate, a champion for the underdog she often felt herself to be. Someone who would know the girl whose thoughts ran so deep, but who covered it up with outrageous play—in order to cover up how much she hurt.

I wanted to be able to trust, but I had lost even more of my ability and desire to trust a man. Yet as scary and unpredictable as men were, it would be better to join their ranks than to be a woman.

By the time I was fifteen, I already believed all that. And it was just my sophomore year in high school.

Dinner and a Movie

When I was in high school I worked as a volunteer at one of the hospitals in town—a candy striper, as they're known in most places, but we called ourselves "Pink Darlings." I learned to make a great chocolate malt working in their snack bar. And I was often put in charge of the skits for our social gatherings, like the Mother-Daughter Tea and the Father-Daughter Box Supper.

My dad didn't have to go with me to those Pink Darling Father-Daughter dinners, but he did, and we always had a good time. We sat with my friends and their fathers, all eating the suppers that our mothers had prepared for us to bring in the shoeboxes we girls had decorated. I loved those nights with my dad although I never told him. By the time we began going to those dinners, it was foreign to me to talk to him about much of anything, much less how I really felt about him.

Those dinners were a mix of exhilaration at the thought of going somewhere, just my dad and me, and apprehension of not knowing quite what to expect from him.

Except for the usual grumpy questions about what he was supposed to wear.

"Do I have to wear a tie?"

Sometimes he asked purely to tease, but there are many times he was truly upset at being told he had to wear a suit and tie to an event—usually one of mine. A PTA program or a piano recital. A play. A band concert. I grew up in the era when people dressed up a lot more than they do now. Men wore suits and ties to church, to most jobs, even when they boarded an airplane. I was taught that taking pride in your appearance was a sign of respect for yourself, the occasion, and the person who was performing.

I hated those conversations between my mom and dad. My mom insisting that he wear a tie, and my dad griping about how uncomfortable they were and how ridiculous he thought it was that he had to wear one. Meanwhile, I'm in my room getting dressed, listening to the argument through the thin walls between our bedrooms. All I heard was that my father thought it was a pain to have to go to my events.

No matter how the argument between my parents went, when it came time to leave, my father was always dressed exactly as he was "supposed" to be. I always thought he looked quite handsome.

I remember one outing more than any other. The time he took me to dinner and a movie, just the two of us.

Like the true Texans that we are, we ate a lot of beef. Most of the time we had a side of beef in a deep freezer, and hardly a day went by that we didn't have some part of a cow to eat. When we splurged for someone's birthday or a special occasion, it always included a trip to a steak place. That's where my dad took me on the only night that my father and I ever did anything by ourselves that wasn't one of those planned events for girls and their dads.

My mother had gone to Dallas with my aunt who owned a dress shop to an event where the fashion retailers sold their new seasonal line of clothing. Usually my dad and I went with them. But this time, for some reason, my dad and I stayed home, and had an entire evening planned out. I couldn't wait. I pushed away the fear that something might happen to trigger his anger, a fear that never left my stream of consciousness.

I didn't need to spend a lot of time figuring out what to wear. I put on my navy blue gabardine dress pants and a pale yellow, scoop-necked, capped-sleeve fitted T-shirt with criss-crossed tennis rackets across the chest.

Daddy took me to one of the nicest steak places in town, where flickering candles sat on tables covered with white tablecloths and set with cloth napkins. The experienced waitresses looked crisp and professional in their gold uniforms and beehive hairdos.

I had been nervous beforehand wondering what we would talk about, worried that we would just sit there and look at each other. Yet as soon as the waitress took our orders, I found myself telling him the things I would have told my mother if she had been there. I told him about my day at school—who said what, and what happened in a class, and why I didn't like so-and-so. He heard those things most nights, so it wasn't like this was anything new. But the difference was, if we had been at home, and my mother was there, she and I would be the only ones talking. My dad would be reading the paper or watching TV.

Most often, it was my mother who responded to me, who acknowledged what I was saying, who knew and remembered what was going on in my daily interactions with friends and teachers and assignments. I think my dad tried, but he seemed to remember football scores and basketball players' records a lot better than he could remember some of the kids who were in band with me. Or what kind of music I liked.

But on this one night it was just the two of us, and at sixteen I didn't care what he spilled and I didn't care how much noise he made when he chewed. And when we finished our dinner, we decided not to get dessert because we were going to the movie and we'd get popcorn and candy there.

The movie was at the cinema in Parker Square, the brand new theatre in town where lots of the kids I went to school with hung out on a Friday night. We saw a movie that wasn't all that great, but I couldn't have cared less, because I was sitting there in a movie theatre with my daddy, eating popcorn and M&Ms and drinking Dr Pepper, listening to him tell me stories. Like when he got sick on Dr Pepper once and never drank it after that. And about the time when he was in the navy and he and his buddies went to a double-feature and he went to sleep. When they got up to walk out, his foot was asleep, and the MPs followed him out because they thought he was drunk.

I treasured that evening with my daddy, so glad to finally have a story of his to keep in my heart.

Likes Girls

The first time I remember my stomach doing little flips over a girl was in the spring of my sophomore year in high school.

The school day ended with the worst class of all, geometry, which followed the health class where the boys harassed me every day. Not a great combination. It didn't help that I didn't understand anything in that class all year. I'd never felt so stupid at school. Usually I was one of the smartest kids in the class. But now, in this sea of people who seemed to understand theorems and proofs better than I did, I felt like an idiot. Humiliated. I made a C on my report card every six weeks for the entire year. I'd never made a C before in my life.

Our teacher was a kind woman who never raised her voice. If you said you didn't understand something, she simply went through the problem again, repeating the same exact explanation that you didn't understand the first time. However, she always complimented me on my homework assignments, writing at the top how beautiful the diagrammed proofs were. They were wrong, but they were beautiful.

My desk was at the very back of the classroom, second row from the door. A new kid named David sat across from me. David had long blond hair like some teenage surfer, with green eyes and a sweet smile. He was one of those kids who looked like he would be too cool to speak to you, but once he opened his mouth, he was as goofy as everybody else. We talked every day as students were coming into class, and if we finished our work early, we talked some more. I don't think he knew any more about geometry than I did, so that made it nice. I didn't ever tell anybody, but I liked David. You know, I liked him, liked him.

Another boy who sat near me was Neil, one of my friends from band. He was quiet and sweet, and he went to another Church of Christ in town. I always liked Neil, but as a friend. He and I loved to crack each other up with Helen Keller jokes. I think Neil understood geometry better than I did. Maybe he could've helped me with it if I'd asked. But I couldn't let him know I didn't understand. It was too embarrassing.

The person who probably could've helped me the most sat across from Neil. She always understood what we were doing. Whenever the teacher called on her, she had the right answer. When she diagrammed the problem on the board, she got it right. Every paper the teacher passed back to her had an A on it.

I always felt awkward talking to Shelli. I didn't know much about her except that she was a year ahead of me in school and that she was a Pink Darlings hospital volunteer like me. I hadn't worked a hospital shift with Shelli, but I'd seen her at the meetings in her pink-and-white gingham jumper that looked just like mine.

Well, it looked a little bit like mine. She looked different in her uniform somehow. Or at least I thought so. For starters, she had a waist.

Shelli wasn't one of those strikingly beautiful girls, but she had an elegant, graceful, and confident presence about her that instantly drew you in. She moved with long, slender limbs and flawless posture, as though she had begun ballet lessons shortly after taking her first step. Her eyes matched the color of her dark brown hair. I thought everything about her was cute.

Since she was a year ahead of us, I don't think Shelli knew a lot of people in our class. She never went out of her way to initiate a conversation with anybody sitting nearby, but if you talked to her first, she responded and was always nice. She maintained a quiet reserve and sensitive strength that mystified me.

I don't think I ever had a conversation with her that amounted to anything. I was too bashful around her to engage in much more than small talk. Sometimes when I was talking to Neil, I'd show off discreetly, never revealing that it was her I was secretly trying to make laugh. On those rare occasions when she grinned or chuckled at something I said, my heart pounded and it felt like I wasn't going to be able to breathe. I worked hard at playing it cool, lest she figure out how badly I craved her attention and her approval. Or how desperately I wanted to fit in with a girl of her caliber.

If I'd been brave enough to start talking to her, maybe I could've had a really sweet friend. But I didn't believe she'd want to talk to me, let alone consider being friends with me.

I wasn't alarmed by the feelings of being strangely drawn to this girl, but I did feel extremely uncomfortable and awkward around her. I didn't know how to act. I didn't feel anything sexual. I had no desire to kiss her, to touch her, to hold her hand—none of those things. But the fact is, whether or not I had feelings of sexual attraction to this girl, the fact that I was drawn to Shelli pointed to a deeper need that wasn't being met. The need to feel competent as a female. To know what that meant, let alone how to accomplish it.

Lots of people might tell me that I was simply experiencing my first crush on a girl. That the feelings pointed to what was blossoming into a sexual orientation that would lead me to be physically attracted to women. Left unspoken and unexplored, that's certainly how it played out. What I really wish, though, is that someone could have realized how afraid and ashamed I was of being female, and how embarrassed and inadequate I felt about doing those things which I believed "made me a girl."

I'll bet someone told Shelli she was pretty.

And I'll bet no one ever called her "son."

Funny Girl

I was the funny girl in high school. You know the one. The girl who made wisecracks in class, played pranks on friends and in classrooms where the teacher wouldn't get mad. The girl who got her photo in the yearbook as the "Class Clown."

I wrote a humor column for our student newspaper and co-authored an "underground" satirical newsletter that went out to hundreds of band students. Whatever *Saturday Night Live* skit character was most popular at the time, you can bet that I was doing an impersonation, even to the extent of learning to play the banjo so that I could do Steve Martin routines.

I thought it was better to let people see only the life-of-the-party girl, the one who could make everybody laugh. It seemed to please people, my mom in particular, and becoming known as a crazy, zany, off-the-wall funny girl who didn't have a serious bone in her body was a big part of the way I was learning to fit in with my peers.

That part of my personality was encouraged to develop to the exclusion of the other more introverted and bashful side. I saw the introverted part of me that was quiet, tender, compassionate, and deeply spiritual as belonging to femininity and weakness. I also kept the serious, thoughtful side in seclusion for fear that anyone who saw those traits might also discover the deep pain that Mama had told me to keep secret.

I was the girl who was different and I liked that. I was unique, and it was fine to be unique.

I was the girl who wore Levi 501 buttonfly jeans before they became popular and a newsboy cap or some other hat, when other girls wouldn't dare mess up their hair with such. The way I dressed didn't completely reject my femininity, but didn't completely embrace it either. I wasn't "Pat" the androgynous character from *Saturday Night Live*. I wasn't at all a tomboy, even though I often looked like one. When it came time to dress up for prom or for church, I looked like the other girls.

Still, the way I dressed on a day-to-day basis, the mannerisms I developed, and the way I presented myself all told people who I was and largely affected how girls related to me, as well as boys.

Along the way I had accumulated lots of girlfriends. Sweet girls who were smart and well mannered, who came from good families. Friends who were good to me, who invited me to their parties. But I was never in a pack of tight friends. I wanted a Laverne and Shirley friendship. I wanted a sister. Someone who looked at me in the same way. Truth is, I did find friendships like that at times in my life, especially in college, but by that time I was holding back. I didn't believe I was worthy. I didn't believe that anyone I'd choose to be my Shirley would want me to be her Laverne.

I wanted what my friends LeeAnn and Elizabeth had when we were in high school. They were best friends and had been for a long time. I worked with LeeAnn on the student newspaper, and we did announcements over the PA system together in the mornings for different organizations, and we became known for coming up with skits to promote some event at school. LeeAnn's friend, Elizabeth, often got in on the planning sessions for those skits, and we'd have so much fun, the three of us sitting at my house working up new routines. We spent more time cracking ourselves up than getting work done.

I loved the days that they rushed me out to one of their cars at lunchtime and we made a mad dash all the way to Taco Burrito (our hometown version of Mexican indigestion)—a fast ten minutes' drive from our school. We only had twenty-five minutes for lunch, giving us just enough time to drive there at breakneck speed, go through the drive-thru, and scarf down a bean burrito and a Dr Pepper before we got back to school for our next class.

Wherever we went, either LeeAnn or Elizabeth drove, the other one in the passenger seat, while I hung over the backseat. They always dropped me off at my house first, and I knew they would, because they were best friends. They dropped the third wheel off first. I didn't mind that, because they never ever treated me as a third wheel.

But since I didn't know how to make and develop friendships, I covered my insecurity with silly antics. Like what I did with Molly, a girl I met at church. She was a year behind me in school, had an incredible soprano voice, and sang in A Cappella, the top choir at our high school. Molly was a strikingly beautiful girl. At church camp the summer before, they dressed her up as Wonder Woman for a skit; she could've passed for Lynda Carter's twin.

Molly didn't seem to fit in with the youth group or have a lot of friends at school. Becoming friends with Molly was partly a result of my seeking out the kids who didn't quite fit in. But I was also mesmerized by this girl who had qualities I admired. And wonder of wonders, she wanted to be friends with me. She appeared to need a friend as much as I did, but remained aloof enough to remain a challenge, and not scare me off.

One Sunday after the evening youth group meeting, we found a ring in the church parking lot. It was a man's costume jewelry, black onyx ring in a fake gold setting. Since our school colors were black and gold, it looked almost identical to the guys' senior class rings. I took the ring and wrote a capital "R" for Rider, the name of our school, in gold glitter glue on the onyx. I then wrapped twine around the band like the girls did who were going steady with a guy to make the large rings fit their fingers.

The next time a bunch of us in the youth group were hanging out somewhere, I made this big production out of asking Molly if she would wear my ring. She said yes. From that night on, this "going steady" became a pretend relationship that we all joked about. The "relationship" went on for quite some time, and we staged fights and break-up scenes, only to be reunited later. It was all an act—a big joke—that was completely out in the open. There was nothing sexual about the game. In fact, I had no sexual attraction to her whatsoever.

My crazy personality, the way I always made a joke out of things, the uniqueness of my dress and relating to people, my being friendly and including everyone, kept anybody from suspecting anything beyond a bunch of high school silliness. And not that they should have suspected anything between Molly and me. What I wish someone had realized at the time was how uncomfortable I felt in my role as a girl.

When I started this game I didn't expect that playing this role—being on this side of the ring—would make me feel comfortable and good in a way that I'd never felt before.

For the first time I experienced what it was like to take the lead in a relationship—even though it was fake. I got to initiate and define the relationship. I got to do the asking. It was a lot better than waiting around until some guy asked me out. A lot better than having to guess at whether or not he "liked me, liked me." I got to say how I felt and ask her if she liked me, too. I was in control.

There were boys I liked, but I had never learned the secret code that signals to a guy that you're interested in him as more than a friend. I never learned how to flirt, and I didn't know where I was supposed to pick that up. Underneath that fact was a thick layer of not believing they'd want me in return. I felt totally at a loss.

And what happened at our cross-town rival game that year surely didn't help.

That fall, all the while the game of going steady with Molly was going on, I was actually dating Kenneth, the boy I'd had a crush on for years and had gone to the band banquet with. Although we now attended cross-town rival high schools, we went out almost every weekend. We ate popcorn and Sugar Babies at the movies and drank Dr Pepper. After the movie we'd head out to Pizza Planet where we ordered a pizza to go and took it home to share with my parents before they went to bed. And then he and I stayed up to watch *Saturday Night Live*.

The biggest football game of the year happened in November. For both our schools, that game was even bigger than homecoming because of the strong tradition of rivalry. The whole town got excited over this game, but it was really a big deal if you were a student. Especially if you were a girl.

Girl status in 1978 was measured by mums. On this particular game day, if you didn't have a mum, that said a lot about your ranking in girldom. I had nothing to worry about that year, though. I was getting a mum. Kenneth had already ordered it from the best florist in town. The florist decorated the corsage with cowbells and little plastic gold footballs and megaphones and the number 79 for our class year. Two streamers hung down in front of all the other clutter, one with your name written in gold glitter and next to it another one with his name. These streamers were the most important features of the mum.

The more stuff the florist put on that thing, the more expensive it was, and the more expensive it was, the more important you were to the boy. Wearing that mum was a sign you wore on your chest all day at school, confirming that somebody "likes you, likes you"—and that they were proud to let everyone know.

As much as I liked the way it felt giving Molly a ring and pretending that we were going together, I loved the fact that this boy I liked was giving me a mum.

I'd been out a couple nights before the game, practicing for the pep rally skit. I'd just gotten home when the phone rang. It was Kenneth. In a short conversation that came out of nowhere, he explained to me that he had been at a youth group devotional that night and had decided that he needed to date a girl from his own church instead of me.

I knew her. She was a girl from band who I had been friends with since my freshman year. He tried to explain that because I went to a different church things wouldn't work out between us.

Stunned over his sudden decision, I didn't really pay a lot of attention to what he was saying. A part of me shut down. Another window in the house of me closed.

That Friday at the pep rally I stood outside the gym, waiting to perform our skit. I looked through the door at the streamers and balloons, the football team striding in wearing their gold double-knit shirts and tight jeans, and the cheerleaders working all 2,500 students into a frenzy, the sea of black and gold going wild to the tune of our fight song.

As I looked at the band, I caught a clear view of my mum on that other girl's chest. It wasn't her fault. I wasn't mad at her. I did want to see if he'd had the florist change the name on the streamer, but I never got close enough.

Christmas

I loved Christmas growing up. I loved Christmas even more than my birthday, and that was saying something. I always felt special on my birthday—from the moment I opened my eyes until I went to bed that night. Every year my mother made me a carrot cake, my favorite, with cream cheese icing, colored frosting scalloped along the edges, and "Happy Birthday Sally!" written across the top. It was as though the world were celebrating its being a better place because I was in it. Even if it was just once a year.

As much as I loved my birthday, there was so much more to enjoy about Christmas. It was a whole season of traditions and celebration. Every part of it was special. It meant standing in line in the cold to go inside the miniature house at Parker Square that was decorated like Santa's house at the North Pole. Then to sit on Santa's lap and tell him what you wanted for Christmas. It meant drinking wassail that the store clerk served you when you went shopping at McClurkan's department store. It meant hearing Muzak Christmas carols in every store and seeing tinsel decorations on the light posts downtown. It meant special treats that you never got to eat at any other time of year.

Just as my mother made every part of my birthday special, she tried to make every part of Christmas special as well. Decorating our Christmas tree was an all-night affair. Every year as we set up the tree, my mother told the story of how her dad made a stand for their Christmas tree out of sawed-off two-by-fours and nailed them directly into the hardwood floor of their living room, much to the dismay of my grandmother. Mama told us how my grandfather flocked the tree with this sticky stuff that made the tree look like it had snow on the branches, but it made a mess everywhere that my grandmother complained about having to clean up.

After my dad set our tree up in the stand, he went back to the den and watched TV. My mother and I put Christmas records on the hi-fi and spent the rest of the night decorating the tree.

Once the strands of lights had been woven evenly through the tree, it was time to start hanging the ornaments on the branches. That was my favorite part. While we painstakingly unwrapped each ornament, my mom told me the stories behind each one. Where it came from, when she bought it, or who gave it to her. There was the box of glass ornaments shaped like bells purchased during World War II, and the basket-weave ornaments that had hung on my grandmother's Christmas tree. In Mama's stories I learned about the history that affected not only the world, but my world, my family, and I began to see how the story of my family fit into a larger story. I learned about the hardships of war in those conversations, from stories about shortages of raw materials like rubber and precious metals determining what kinds of Christmas decorations could be made and sold.

The last thing we placed on the tree was the angel purchased for my first Christmas. Once the angel was placed on top of the tree and the cardboard manger scene sat at the base, our Christmas tree was complete. We turned on the tree lights, then sat down on the couch with a cup of hot spiced tea and one of the treats my mom had baked. I took in all that surrounded me through each of my senses—the smell of old boxes stored in the attic and cinnamon and cloves from the tea, the raucous voices of the Chipmunks followed by the Ray Conniff singers belting carols from the hi-fi, the taste of sweet that only my mother could bake, the warmth of a fire in the fireplace, the tree perfect with its tinsel and glow of lights.

Every now and then my dad would walk past the living room on his way to the bathroom and stop to check our progress. He never stayed, even if we tried to entice him with snacks. He turned up his nose at the mention of drinking anything hot and seemed bored by the whole process of decorating the tree. In later years I learned that his father had never participated in any part of celebrating Christmas, so he grew up believing men didn't do that. But when I was growing up, I didn't know that, and so I believed he'd rather watch TV or read the newspaper than spend time with my mother and me. My father's attitude every Christmas added to my belief that he didn't like me enough to do those things just to be with me. Just because I liked them. I wanted him to do things I liked in the same way I went to football games and basketball games because it was something he liked and I wanted to be with him.

I wanted my dad to do these things especially at Christmas. He made the money that bought all the presents and all the snacks and all the wrapping paper and all the material things that were associated with Christmas. He put the lights up on the outside of the house. But I would've given anything to have him decorate the tree with us, to sing Christmas carols with him in Chipmunk voices, to wrap presents with him. To fix him a cup of tea and a plate of special cookies and hear him say how good it all was. To hear his stories about Christmas. So I could learn the other half of who I was.

As I grew older Christmas became more stressful, because I learned that there were lots of things about Christmas that were difficult for my family. For my dad, especially. Particularly if we had to spend time with his side of the family. We didn't see my father's family very much even though they lived only fifty miles away.

His older brother never grew past the differences of childhood to embrace my dad. My dad's older sister hadn't been abusive, but she was equally distant. I never felt comfortable with these grandparents who seemed more like strangers. I have no memory of ever sitting on their laps, of them hugging me or showing any affection to me. The only Christmas gift I remember receiving from them was a red metal toy tractor, like you would've given a small boy. I was nine. And I was a girl.

I think it must've been hard for my dad to keep trying to go back to a family where he wasn't wanted and never felt like he fit in. When I was little, we occasionally drove over there to see them at Christmas or on other occasions, and he tried. We all did. But it was always strained, and every time we left, my dad wasn't quite the same. He might be quiet and distant on the drive home. Sometimes he became angry, and sometimes it escalated into a fit of rage and he threatened to stop the car and make us get out.

My heart pounded and my mind raced, frantically trying to figure out where my mother and I could go and what we would do all alone in the dark on the highway. Mama did her best to keep her composure and de-escalating the fit. And I believed his anger was solely directed at my mother and me.

Visits to my father's family were often followed by visits to my mother's family, the only family I really knew. Spending time with my mother's parents, her siblings and their families, were good times, sweet times, filled with people I saw genuinely loving my father. And he seemed to genuinely love them.

Adding to the stress of travel, of packing and driving and arguing over when we had to leave, the financial stress of buying presents and groceries to have all the extra holiday goodies made Christmas an exhausting season. With each passing year, I became more aware that this was a volatile time, and I grew more and more anxious about the possibility of Christmas being ruined.

In 1976, when I was fifteen, I wished there hadn't been any Christmas.

Like most Christmases, we planned to spend the actual holiday with my mother's sister's family. We arrived the day before Christmas Eve so that my mother and I could help my aunt in her dress shop on one of the store's busiest days of the year. As it got closer to closing time, business began to slow, so my aunt and I became intensely involved in a round of "Speed," a rapid-fire card game that required all of one's attention.

It was dark outside when I heard the bell on the front glass door. I looked up to see my father standing in the cold, damp night air in nothing but a white undershirt—no jacket, no sweater. His face was as white as a sheet and his eyes looked as though they'd pop right out of his head. I instantly knew that he was enraged. The world stopped. There was no more Speed. There was no more Christmas Eve. No more Christmas. No more peace in my world. The life drained from my body and I wished the earth would open up and swallow me, because I knew what was coming. I didn't want to go through this again. One minute I'm happy and life is innocent, it's Christmas Eve, and everyone's together, and the next minute all hell has broken loose with no explanation as to what went wrong.

I can't express how many times I had felt that way in my fifteen years and how deeply I dreaded and despised those moments that came so abruptly. I was terrified again, and in the next few hours I'd be more terrified than I'd ever been in my life.

My father began to rant and my mother tried to find out what had happened, but in his rage the story made little sense. She continued to try to get him to calm down, but it was no use. When he got like this, the best thing to do was to stay out of his way. He couldn't be rational.

He told my mother that he was leaving and if we wanted to go with him we needed to get our things from the house. Then we were to meet him at some store on the way out of town where he'd wait until we got there. But not for long.

The details of what happened next are a blur. Somehow all our presents were taken from under the Christmas tree and loaded back into our car while my mom and I packed our suitcases.

With that done, my uncle took me back to the master bedroom. I sat on the bed while he sat on a chair. As he told me I had to be strong for my mother, the situation became even more serious since I don't think my uncle had ever talked specifically to me. Through all the holidays and vacations, through all the summers I had come and stayed with them, he had never once had a conversation with just me. But that night he felt it important enough to take me aside to tell me what had happened.

He told me that my grandmother had been sitting at the kitchen table when she said something and my father got mad. The situation escalated into a horrible fight in which he lunged at her, and in an attempt to defend herself she threw a scalding cup of coffee on him, and he attacked her. My uncle came in and pulled them apart. Now my father was waiting for us at a store miles away from the house. In the cold. Without a coat. On Christmas Eve.

When we pulled up to the store, he came bursting out the door in that white undershirt, all the color drained from his face and his bulging eyes full of rage. He opened the door, damp from sweat and freezing drizzle. For an instant I felt pity for him. Pity turned to terror as he got in the car and started raging. I wanted to jump out of the car and run back to my aunt and uncle and cousins and grandmother. If my mother hadn't been in the car, I would have. At that moment I would gladly have stayed anywhere than spend the next two-and-a-half hours in a car with my father.

My mother tried without success to get him to stop, to just wait, not to drive in that condition, assuring him we didn't have to go back to her sister's house, but to stay in the parking lot and not drive until he calmed down. He ignored her and took off out of the parking lot and onto the highway like a madman. My heart was beating so hard I thought it would rise up out of my throat. My breath became so rapid and so shallow that at one point I thought if I didn't put my head down between my knees I'd surely faint. But I didn't dare move or change position for fear of calling attention to myself. I avoided eye contact in the rearview mirror, lest the expression of fear on my face be mistaken for defiance and provoke more anger. I wanted to disappear.

Daddy raged the whole way home, screaming obscenities about the only family I knew, about the grandparents I loved, saying such horrible things that it took everything in me to keep from screaming back in their defense. But I said nothing, for I had learned by the age of fifteen that responding only made it worse. I had learned that you couldn't have a rational conversation with my father when he was in this state of mind. And when he was in a calmer state of mind, no one ever brought the pain of these moments up again, for fear of what it might trigger, and because none of us knew how to talk about what had happened.

So I sat there and endured the ranting and the threats that he was going to "stop the g-d car and make you two bitches get out and walk!"

I prayed. I was furious and I was terrified, so I prayed. I prayed to a God whom I believed loved me and didn't like what was happening in that car any more than I did. I prayed without making a sound because my mother had taught me I could always talk to God, no matter where I was, no matter who I was with, no matter what was going on around me. She had taught me that I didn't have to say a word out loud, I could just think it and God was close enough to hear my prayer. So I asked God to just get us home.

I asked God to make him stop, like I did every day of my life.

I don't know what time we got home. I don't have any recollection about the rest of that night. But I remember Christmas day like it was yesterday.

My mother tried desperately to go ahead and have Christmas morning just like we'd always done, but it wasn't the same without my cousins and grandmother. Part of me was terrified to go in the living room. I didn't know what state of mind my father would be in, and I knew from past episodes that in those first few days anything could trigger another round of raging. Part of me was angry with my dad for having ruined Christmas, for making us leave the rest of the family. I was mad at him for hurting my grandmother and for talking to my mother and me like we were nothing. I was mad at him for scaring me. Again. And yet part of me ached for him to come back. To come back from wherever he went during those times.

This shell of a man who looked exactly like my father sat on the end of the couch that morning reading a newspaper as though it was like every other day, and never spoke to us. We handed out the presents like we always did on Christmas morning, so we could take turns opening them one at a time and see what everyone else got. We put all of his presents in front of him on the floor, but he wouldn't open them. He wouldn't even acknowledge that we were in the room.

That was the year that I got a banjo and a 1977 calendar that had every week marked with my lesson at the music store. There was a tag on a small square box that said "To Sally from Daddy." I couldn't wait to open it. Maybe he'd respond to this, I thought. My heart pounded as I opened the package he had wrapped himself—a rarity. That spring I was going to take Driver's Ed, so Daddy had bought me a keychain, an oversized letter "S" made out of reddish brown leather and had keys to both cars put on it. As I pulled the keys out of the box, I began to tear up, and I went over to where he was sitting on the couch and sat on the floor in front of him. "Thank you, Daddy, thank you for the keys," I said shaking with emotion, partly fear.

I wanted him to simply put the paper down and say that he was sorry. Then we would all cry and hug and start Christmas all over. Even if it was just the three of us, it would be okay. But he didn't. My father sat there behind the newspaper, holding it at an angle so that I could clearly see his expressionless face as he continued reading the sports page while I thanked him for the key ring.

Daddy never said a word while we were opening presents, nor did he speak to me the rest of the day. In fact, it was nearly February before he spoke to me again.

That afternoon my mother and I found a very nice restaurant that was open Christmas Day. We had turkey and dressing with giblet gravy and cranberry sauce, sweet potatoes, and pumpkin pie. Under any other circumstances, it would've been the finest of meals, but I didn't care if I ate or not. I did eat. And I carried on conversation with my mother although I didn't want to talk. As hard as my mother tried to make everything okay, that was the most miserable meal I have ever experienced.

When school started after New Year's, I paid attention in class, did my homework, played with my friends. We went to church and I was active in the youth group. But I never told a soul.

Slowly my father came back to us, as he always did. After a few days, he retreated into a calmer silence, still not participating as part of the family, but at least he was no longer prone to rage. In this instance, because the episode had been so traumatic, it took longer for him to calm down and not fly off into a rage again.

It was February before my father came to a place to make things right with my grandmother. It was a joyous moment when we all three got in the car and drove to Archer City to visit her. I don't remember what he said to her or what she said in return, but I remember their tears. He hugged her and she hugged him and at that moment I felt the concrete slab I'd carried in my chest the last two months break away. Everything was okay again.

It was always best right after these episodes; everybody was so happy to be back as a family again, back like we were supposed to be. Except my mom. With every episode it took her longer to come back, to respond sweetly to my dad again. I wanted her to, though. I wanted everyone to get along. To love each other. Not to be stuck in this vicious cycle of peace, uneasiness, rage, and silence.

When we got home that night from visiting my grandmother, I went to my dresser and pulled out the box my dad had given me for Christmas. And even though I couldn't drive yet, the next day I took my keys to school for the very first time.

College Sophomore

Today people believe the awareness of same-sex attraction happens at a young age, but for me—being the late bloomer that I was—I didn't realize what was happening until my sophomore year in college.

When I had a dream about a girl.

In my dream I was sitting in the front seat of my car at a drive-in movie with Pam Dawber, one of the stars of *Mork & Mindy*, the popular TV sit-com from the late 1970s and early 1980s. In many ways, it was a perfectly sweet and innocent dream, with a twist: Pam and I were on a date and I was the boy. Right before I woke up from the dream, I leaned over and kissed her. On the lips.

The dream frightened me. Partly because I was me, but I was a boy. Partly because of how my heart had raced in anticipation of that sweet little innocent peck of a kiss. Partly because it felt so right.

I wondered why I dreamt something like that. What did it mean?

The next morning over breakfast in the campus cafeteria, I told my friends about the dream. After all, it couldn't possibly mean what I thought it could mean.

Could it?

Besides, I reassured myself, I was dating a boy. A boy I really liked.

In 1980 nobody talked about homosexuality. Except when it was mentioned as a vile abomination in a sermon at church. Or to make fun of some guy who was over-the-top flamboyant with effeminate mannerisms. Ellen DeGeneres hadn't come out yet. The AIDS epidemic hadn't yet forced us to pay attention. Sure, Archie Bunker and Frank Burns had been making snide comments on popular TV shows like *All in the Family* and *MASH* for several years. But society as a whole kept any discussion contained, and the church alternated between choking silence and hateful condemnation. So, no one in my circle of friends would make such an assumption, let alone an accusation, about me. That possibility wasn't on our radar screen.

I made a joke out of the dream and everyone laughed. It was a group joke for a couple of weeks and I egged it on. Since I was the funny girl, everyone attributed what I told them to my outrageous sense of humor.

What I didn't tell them was how the dream made me feel. I didn't tell them that I enjoyed the kiss more than I had enjoyed any kiss from a boy, and even more, how right it felt to be this masculine version of myself. I felt more comfortable—safer, more secure, more confident—living out of this masculine persona than I did living as a girl.

There had been other times when I'd felt that same way. When I played dress up wearing Daddy's clothes. In the third grade on Western Day, the one day out of the year when girls were allowed to wear pants to school. I got to wear jeans, boots, and a cowboy shirt. Another time was in my senior year of high school when I pretended to "go steady" with Molly. An unexplainable calm had come at those times. I felt more at peace with myself in those clothes. In those roles.

At nineteen I hadn't even begun to realize what it was I was wrestling with. I didn't realize I was experiencing homosexual attractions, because at the same time I wanted nothing less than to be in a dating relationship with a boy I was very much attracted to. A boy I was excited to spot in the campus center or when he called me in my dorm room at night. A boy I spent hours fantasizing about.

So many experiences had solidified the beliefs I had about myself. The beliefs that had started forming long before my sophomore year of college, beliefs about my worth and value as a female, about my desirability to a man, about my ability to fit in, to be "one of the girls," and ultimately, about where I found comfort and safety—about where I felt most wanted and loved.

At nineteen I still believed that someday marriage wouldn't seem so scary. Maybe the right guy really would take all those fears away, and I would end up like most of the women I'd known in my life, being some man's wife, some child's mother. But the picture was awfully blurry. And I had no idea how I would get there. Or if I even really wanted to.

In Love with a Boy

Eddie.

I know exactly where I was standing the day we met. I know what we were wearing on that Sunday morning at church when a mutual friend introduced us.

We were in Sing Song together, so we hung out after practice and got to be friends. We made late-night runs before curfew to Larry's Better Burger where they made homemade ice cream. Or we ate at Harry Jordan's, a family style restaurant, with a group of friends after church on Sunday. He wrote to me over that summer, but it wasn't until the next fall that we actually went on a date.

On our first date he took me to one of his fraternity socials, picking me up in his brother's stick-shift Volkswagen Beetle. We went dressed in costume for the party's theme and had a great time with his friends, playing and acting silly.

I went to bed that night feeling completely giddy from having been with a boy I really liked. The next morning I found a card from him waiting for me at our campus post office. As I read it, a warmth filled me. I felt wanted, valued, and appreciated by a boy I really liked. I was excited for the rest of the day.

Thoughts of him consumed my every moment. There was the mystery of whether or not this would continue and progress. Questions about what he was thinking and experiencing. An awkwardness of being in the beginning phase of a new relationship, not quite sure what it was yet. Giddy with excitement over what it could become, thrilled to feel that way about a boy. I'd been in that place before with Kenneth, but back then, as young as I was, those emotions were purely "puppy love." After all, I was only thirteen. Back then my every thought was about Kenneth. I could turn any conversation toward something about Kenneth.

I'd also had those feelings with another boy, one I met at church camp. I thought he felt the same about me only to have him start calling me "sister." I wanted to remind him that you don't kiss your sister the way he'd kissed me, but I said nothing and settled into the role it seemed boys continually placed me—a sister, a pal, a confidante, but never the romantic lead.

Eddie was different.

He was the boy I thought would be the one to clear up all the confusion I had about relationships between men and women, about marriage.

Throughout the times we spent together, there were no serious conversations, no "define the relationship" talk, nothing beyond a playful peck of a kiss; but my heart became deeply invested in him in a way that I'd never allowed myself before. I liked being with somebody I was connected to, somebody who wanted to be with me like I wanted to be with him.

Or at least I thought so.

Perhaps most people think the absence of a real kiss should've tipped me off, but naïve as I was, I honestly thought he was being a real gentleman.

That year I waited for him to pick me up for the Homecoming game, but he never showed up. I was in the band, so I had to go on to the game, mum-less again. I spotted him in the crowd during the third quarter. He never sought me out to explain what happened until later that night when he showed up at my dorm, mum box in hand, telling me he'd been up the previous night preparing for his fraternity breakfast and was so tired that he slept through the game.

I never told him that I'd seen him there. That I knew he was lying.

He invited me to go on a ski trip over Christmas break with his fraternity. When I showed up to ride with him, he had decided to ride with another guy, and I was forced to ride with people I hardly knew.

I should have known.

I was young and I wanted to believe that a boy could care for me the way that I cared for him. That eventually God would remove whatever fear, whatever confusion remained within me. But neither of those things happened.

In the spring of our sophomore year Eddie took me to his spring social. When I refused to go dancing at Billy Bob's with his friends after dinner, he'd gotten mad at me. He didn't understand why I wouldn't go dancing with him. I'd been raised all my life to believe dancing was a sin. So I just couldn't go. He got so mad that I ended up riding back to Abilene with my roommate.

After band rehearsal that Monday, he asked me to go to Burger King. To talk. Not a good sign. I got a Whopper, but I didn't get to have it my way.

When he said he only wanted to be friends, I was devastated. However, I played it cool and acted as though I was in complete agreement, that that's what I wanted too, because I never wanted him—or anyone—to know how stupid I felt or how much I'd cared about this boy. How much I'd wanted him to care for me. My fantasies of him had been more than a trip to Six Flags. And until that moment, I was still very much the girl in my fantasies.

After a year of going to each other's fraternity/sorority socials, of him sending me cards and flowers, of dinners and movies and phone calls late at night, I was supposed to just switch off my feelings over lunch. Inside though, I hung on to the possibility that something might come of that relationship since we remained friends beyond that day.

In a much deeper place, I stopped believing there was anything about me that a boy would want in a girlfriend. I felt so incredibly stupid for ever having believed for a moment that one of them might. So incredibly stupid for caring for another man who didn't want me. Like I'd been doing all my life.

And I was tired.

That wasn't the end. There were other boys. Other dates. Other times of trying to feel that way again. But I just couldn't get there.

In Love with a Girl

By the time I was a junior in college, what I wanted most was to be male.

I didn't understand how I got there. How I got from my thoughts being consumed by a boy named Eddie to wanting nothing less than to be in a relationship with a girl.

And yet, a relationship with a girl wasn't what I ultimately wanted. I wanted to be in a relationship with a boy who loved me, wanted me, and cherished me. Didn't I?

In 1982, the thought of two girls being in a romantic relationship was forbidden. In my world, it was the only thing worse than a girl who wasn't married getting pregnant. I didn't want a relationship like that, I told myself over and over. I was only experiencing thoughts about this particular girl in my head as a simple, harmless fantasy that helped me feel less alone, especially at night.

I had always found great comfort inside my thoughts. I first learned to put myself to sleep by creating a whole world in my head. My unusually vivid imagination could recreate everything I heard or read down to the last detail. It made the books I read come alive. As the adults in my life told stories around me, I could instantly picture everything they were saying. With Papa's help, I learned to do the same thing on my own, imagining places I wanted to go, things I wanted to do, people I wanted to be with. Most of all, I could be the person I wanted to be.

When I was in junior high, my relationship fantasies were about Kenneth. Perfectly innocent, sweet daydreams that I created in my thirteen-year-old mind at night while lying in bed. Daydreams about trips to Six Flags with my youth group from church, only in the fantasy I'd invited Kenneth. We rode all the rides together, we stood in line like the other teenage couples I'd watched standing in line summers before, wondering why it was they liked to put their hands in each other's back pockets, and why, when it was so hot, they liked to stand so close, with their arms wrapped around each other. Didn't that make them hotter? My mother always commented on how disgusting that was and how nice girls didn't let boys do things like that.

My ultimate fantasies about Kenneth were limited to putting my arms around him on the log ride as we shot down that last steep slide, right before we splashed into the water and everyone got drenched. Then afterward, sharing a raspberry sherbet on a stick while we walked around the park by ourselves.

So how did I get to this place? I constantly wondered. It couldn't be what I feared, could it? It certainly wasn't the place I fantasized about throughout my life. It's not the place I wanted to be at twenty, at a Christian university. How could this happen to me, a good Christian girl? That only happened to people who are sick. At least that's what my mom said. Or to people who have been so bad and rebellious that they've walked away from God and they don't care about him.

That wasn't me at all. I cared deeply about God.

But I didn't know how to change this desire. I didn't know if I wanted to change it because the thoughts about her made me feel so good. Better than I'd ever felt before. My feelings for a boy had never been that deep or sexually charged, nor had any relationship ever been as emotionally intimate.

From the outside, and certainly from her perspective, what we had was a friendship and nothing more. We were two young women who met and became best friends in college. But somewhere in the spring of our junior year, my feelings changed, as though I woke up one morning and suddenly realized what all the songs on the radio were about—songs about being in love, about not being able to live without this someone. Songs I'd never quite related to before. That's the way I felt—as if I were in love with this girl—but surely couldn't be. It was wrong to feel that way. It was even more wrong to act on those feelings.

I recognized that my feelings for her were romantic. Emotions that I figured must be what I should be experiencing for a boy, but didn't. I knew I could never act on what was going through my head or let anyone know I had those thoughts. I was too embarrassed. Too utterly ashamed.

I wanted to be with her all the time, more than I wanted to be with anyone else. I became awkward and nervous around her, yet felt safer and more connected to her than I'd ever felt with anyone else.

I couldn't tell anyone about any of it. Besides, if I did, I knew it would change everything. And not just my friendship with her. Everything. It's the worst that could happen. At least that's what I'd been told. I'd seen the worlds of my friends whose families found out and their world crumbled around them. I couldn't let that happen to me. I had to keep the secret, like I'd always kept secrets. No one could ever find out. Especially not her.

What would she think of me if she knew? She'd be disgusted. She's not like that. She doesn't have feelings like that for me.

So many times I wondered what I was freaking out about. I hadn't done anything. Dr. Brecheen said in Bible class that it's only wrong if you act on it. And I hadn't acted on it. I would have rather died than act on it.

I just had no idea what to do.

The Principal's Office

I don't remember the first time he called me into his office. Over the five years I taught speech, debate, and theatre at that middle school, I ended up in the principal's office more than I ever did as a student.

Sometimes it was because I hadn't taken attendance or failed to turn in my roll sheet. Or I hadn't marked it correctly and the attendance clerk couldn't make sense of it. No one bothered to explain to me, a green-as-a-gourd new teacher, that Texas public schools derived their funding from the state based on attendance. If they had, perhaps I would've been more diligent about taking attendance. But most of the time I forgot because I was so excited to get started with what we were doing in class that my mind wasn't focused on what I considered administrivia. I just wanted to teach those kids how to get up in front of an audience.

I got in trouble because I was late. Maybe five minutes, maybe two minutes. He knew exactly how many minutes because he stood at my classroom door every morning waiting for me to get there. As soon as I arrived, he looked at his watch, shook his head at me in disgust, and sauntered back to his office—never mind saying hello to me or the herd of twelve-year-olds filing past him to their classrooms. Getting in trouble for being late was never motivation enough for me to get there on time. And the longer I worked there, even though I loved teaching those kids, the more I hated the place, and it became more and more difficult for me to be punctual.

I also got in trouble because I wanted to do things differently, outside the box like the teachers in movies do. It was a little bit comforting that most of the time their principals hated them, too. Besides, there was a lot that I had yet to learn and I made a lot of mistakes. My enthusiasm got the best of me at times, but it also captivated kids and helped them relate to me.

Sometimes I flat messed up. Like the time I was responsible for all the junior high speech events at our spring competition against other schools in our district. One of my seventh graders was about to win the whole competition with his prose cutting from Charles Dickens' *Great Expectations*, until someone pointed out the rule that said this year the seventh graders were supposed to use the work of American authors. I somehow skipped over that technicality. It was a shame, because that kid would've won first place, and the principal was furious with me.

I had been hired to start speech and theatre programs for both the middle school and the high school, and I taught half-days at both schools. I wasn't actually certified to teach theatre, but I'd been in a few plays in high school and college and thought it would be fun to try my hand at directing. Unfortunately, I didn't have the training to know how to work with a facility that was less than adequate. The school district was so small that they didn't have an auditorium for fine arts productions at the high school. The only thing I had to work with was a cafetorium at the middle school, complete with bright white walls and fluorescent lights. I didn't know much about technical theatre, but I knew the backstage area was supposed to be dark, and we needed something besides fluorescent lights. So I called one of my former college professors, a technical theatre director, and asked him to look at the stage and give me some tips as to how we could produce a better show.

My professor was appalled, laughing and shaking his head, saying it would be a miracle if I could do anything with that facility. And that's what he told the middle school principal. I had thought it would be helpful if my principal heard from someone knowledgeable what we needed to do to the stage to make it a more workable, more educational experience for the students. I was wrong.

The next day, the library aide interrupted my seventh grade speech class to tell me that the principal wanted to see me in his office. I was accustomed to being called out of class to go to his office, even though interrupting a teacher in the middle of class wasn't supposed to happen. But this time, since he'd acted receptive to my professor's comments, I naively thought this visit would be different. As a hopeful twenty-five-year-old, I went in convinced that this would be the turning point in our relationship.

"Wipe that dumb grin off your face and sit down," was his greeting as I stood in the open doorway to his office. I was certain both secretaries, whose desks were not ten feet away, heard his comment, and I was embarrassed to death. How foolish of me to retain any hope of pleasing this man. Most any man, I had come to believe. No matter how hard I tried, there was something about me that an overwhelming majority of them didn't like. I didn't know what it was and I was tired of trying to figure it out.

My stomach churned as I sat in a chair across from his desk. The expression on his face, before he ever spoke a word, told me he was mad, and my heart rate increased exponentially. My mouth got dry and I shook all over, like I had shaken all my life in the presence of a man's anger.

Just like I had with my dad.

Just like I had with men in my family.

Just like I had with my high school band directors.

His face turned bright red and he glared at me. "Don't you ever embarrass me like you did yesterday, bringing somebody in to tell me how to do my job. Do you hear?" he bellowed at me from across the desk. "I'll tell you what, you may be an excellent teacher, but I absolutely can't stand you as a person!"

I was baffled by his reaction, because the day before when my professor was there explaining to him that the facility was truly very difficult to work with, my principal appeared to be reasonable and understanding.

"Well, I'm sorry you feel that way," I replied, praying that he wouldn't see how crushed, terrified, and humiliated I was. I turned and walked out of the office.

I had started a tradition of doing a fall production, helping me spot talent for the one act play competition that I directed in the spring to raise money for our fledgling speech and drama budget. My fifth and final year at that middle school I directed an old classic, *You Can't Take It with You*, with a large cast. Lots of students turned out for the auditions. The industrial arts classes helped with some set pieces to hide the white stucco walls of the cafetorium stage, and I asked an electrician friend who had worked with theatrical lighting in college to rig up some lighting so that it would look like a real production.

And it didn't look half bad.

The week before the show, I asked a couple of the boys to clean out the storage room backstage so the actors who had costume changes could use it as a dressing room. I checked it after rehearsal, made sure everything was straightened up, turned out the lights, locked the doors, and went home for the night.

The next morning, the moment I walked into the building, I immediately knew something was wrong. First, the principal wasn't standing at the door waiting to see what time I arrived, and second, the school smelled like smoke.

I walked to the cafetorium in a panic, but when I got there, the set was intact. The big velvet curtain, though, was black with soot, and the brilliant white walls were now a dingy gray. About that time the principal walked up and explained that there hadn't actually been a blaze, just a lot of smoke damage from a short in the wiring. Then he asked me to come into his office. He asked me what had happened during our rehearsal the previous afternoon. I told him everything I could remember, including having the boys clean out the storage room so that we could use it as a dressing room.

It seems that during the process of cleaning out the storage room, the boys leaned two backdrops from a choral performance against a breaker box. The breaker box was there to protect the electrical wiring from coming into contact with anything that might cause a short in the electrical system. That is, unless the box is faulty. The fire chief who came out to inspect the facility the next day explained that the boys did nothing wrong in placing those backdrops where they did. If the box had been working properly, he said, there wouldn't have been a problem.

After the visit from the fire chief, things went back to normal, except for needing to have the proscenium curtain cleaned and the back wall whitewashed.

In the middle of my first class after the chief's visit, the library aide came to sit with the students since I was, again, called to the principal's office. Once I got there, the principal closed the door to his office behind me and handed me some papers, his face a brilliant red. "Notice of Termination" was typed at the top of the first page, followed by a few paragraphs that proceeded to accuse me of arson, of purposely setting fire to the stage, and therefore releasing me from my duties as a teacher.

"You'll need to sign there at the bottom of that second page," he told me, handing me a pen.

"None of that is true and I'm not signing it," I said, trying to keep from stuttering. My heart was pounding and I was shaking all over as I always did, but I wasn't about to sign something that wasn't true. "And besides," I added, "you're not solely responsible for my contract. My contract is handled at the high school."

He came up over the desk at me, furious, shaking his fist at me, telling me I would sign. I leapt up and opened the door to the office because I was scared to death. He came around the desk and bellowed at one of the secretaries to come in. She stood at the door, obviously uncomfortable, not knowing where to look, at him or at me or neither of us. She chose to focus on the papers in my hand. She had been kind to me over the years, watching me go in and out of his office, undoubtedly hearing everything he had said to me. "Trudy," I told her, "I'm not signing those papers because it's not true."

He instructed the secretary to type up some kind of addendum to the document saying that I had refused to sign it.

Meanwhile, I had to go back to my classroom and teach the rest of the day. I had to pretend nothing had happened, as I had done so many times in my life.

As soon as I could, I called the college professor who had supervised my student teaching. After explaining to her what had happened, she immediately went to bat for me, driving home my lifelong belief that women are the ones who take care of you, who are highly competent and emotionally support-ive. My defenders and protectors. Within the week she set up a meeting with him on my behalf, followed by a meeting with the district superintendent. No action was ever taken against me. No one ever apologized. But every day someone made a joke in the teacher's lounge about my being a pyromaniac. One of the teachers finally explained that they were joking about it because the accusation was so ridiculous.

One by one, I stored these types of events in a mental safe deposit box. I was the only one who held the key and knew its contents. As time passed, the box got filled.

At a district debate tournament, I stepped up on behalf of the kids, asking the faculty to announce the debate awards at a ceremony rather than just writing the names of the winners on a chalkboard. Later, when I was alone in the school hallway, the principal of another school grabbed my shoulders and shoved me against the lockers and started to scream at me. "I don't know who you think you are. You are not in charge here so quit telling everybody what to do."

I knew this man was a Christian. We went to the same large church. Our paths didn't directly cross, but I knew he was a member. I saw him serving communion. I heard people talk about him, his family. He was supposed to be my Christian brother who showed me the love of Christ as a fellow believer.

By that time I had come to believe that something about my personality, my voice, my very presence put men off. Because I believed I somehow provoked his response and because I knew him to be a brother in Christ, I felt strongly about trying to make things right with him before I left the tournament that night.

After everything was over, I waited around and went to his office. He was sitting behind his desk and never got up. I said I was sorry and explained why I had made the suggestion to award the kids' medals in front of everyone. He never apologized, never acknowledged any overreaction on his part.

I had no desire to take legal action against either of these principals, though I could have. But that wouldn't have undone the harm. Other instances of male rage against me during those years of teaching helped fill that box. No legal remedy would have kept the lies from being planted even deeper—lies that said men aren't safe and they just don't like you, Sally.

I'm thankful for those who did see my potential. The principal at the high school. Parents of my students. The college professor who had gone to bat for me. And I believe God placed other men in my life at that same time to show me a different picture of masculinity. It's almost warlike, the opposing images of men that were cast before me in my adult years. Along with the prevailing messages that men were not safe, and were uncaring and thoughtless, there were also surprising contrasts. I use the word "surprising," because kind, reasonable, and good men never seemed to be the prevailing norm to me. Quite the opposite. But the surprises were enough to keep me hoping. Hoping that I might be wrong about what I believed about men, about women, about relationships, about myself.

I slipped other events during my ten years of teaching into my deposit box of beliefs.

In the late 1980s, I stood by as friends searched for a young woman kidnapped from the parking lot of the nicest department store at the mall. They found her in a field outside of town, raped and murdered. She'd been attending my Sunday school class after moving to the area to teach elementary school. I didn't know her well, but I had talked to her. I had gone to college with her sister. I'd heard all my life that women had to be careful how they acted around men. But she dressed like me, like the women at my college, and something like that still happened to her.

A few years later, one of my former students, a sweet nineteen-year-old college freshman, had come to visit me during Christmas break where we had a great time laughing and hanging out. A few weeks later she was abducted from her in-between-semesters job at a convenience store. They found her later, also raped and murdered.

These events had a powerful impact on my already fearful view of men, distancing me and shutting me down more inside with each one.

From that point on there were fewer dates with men. I focused on work, putting everything I had into teaching and coaching a successful speech and debate team at a different high school where the female principal was the epitome of competence and intellect and compassion all rolled into one.

Debate tournaments took me away every weekend giving me a convenient excuse for having no social life. In reality, I was desperately lonely. I didn't dare admit that to myself or anyone else, because to me, being lonely was the final recognition that you really weren't wanted.

That was the most hurtful lie I believed. That I wasn't wanted. And never would be wanted by a man.

The Stadium

Sometimes it seems as if all women are connected but me. Like they all know each other and how to be with each other in ways that I don't. They all know hair and makeup and babies and cooking and other marks of femininity that my culture said made you female. The things I don't seem to get. And never have. Like I'm on the periphery of some huge stadium full of girls—the Rose Bowl of girl games. I'm in the parking lot and I can see them and hear them and smell them. Yet somehow I can't find the gate that's unlocked, the one that's supposed to let me in. I want to go in. I want to be one of them.

Or at least, for the longest time I did. And some small part of me—or maybe a large part of me—still does. But it would take some help now. A tutor, maybe? Who will want to tutor a grown woman? Maybe the same type of people who teach adult literacy classes. It's so embarrassing for adults to admit they can't read and to ask someone to teach them. It feels so awkward not to have this skill that everyone else takes for granted, as though it had never occurred to others that someone who's lived half a century still might not know how to do it.

It doesn't matter that I don't know how to do what a lot of women seem to know instinctively, like taking care of babies, or cooking really well, or fixing hair and putting on make-up. My appearance, how I dress, or what gifts I've been given aren't what make me, or anyone else, feminine. But the culture I grew up in said possessing those abilities were, in part, what made you a woman.

In my world, if I don't know about those things, I get left out. The women don't mean to leave me out. But they do.

I haven't had the same life experiences as most of them. I haven't dated a boy whom I fell in love with, got engaged to, and planned a wedding with. I haven't been someone's wife. I haven't had a baby and I haven't cared for a child. No one has ever called me Mama. In my world—the southern world of women who go to church in Texas—the majority of women share those experiences. And if you haven't had them, you can easily get left out. I understand that. It's the common experiences that tend to bond us, and people tend to seek out companions who are most similar to them.

As a result, most women in the stadium don't know I'm there. Others know I'm there, but because they feel like they are limited to the activities inside the stadium, they feel awkward around someone like me.

Then there are lots of women who wave to me from inside the stadium, because they genuinely like and respect me. If you asked them, what I can't do wouldn't matter to them. Some of them even come over to the gate and spend time talking to me. But eventually they go back inside the stadium, where all the action is—where everyone is about the business of being in relationships and raising children.

I think most of us who feel we don't fit in decide at an early age that we don't want to go in the stadium. Or at least we put up a good front. But no little girl wants to feel left out, not invited to the girl party. If she is left out, it can be easier to pretend she didn't want to go in the first place. Then the more you avoid it, the less you know, and the more you feel left out. People begin to believe you don't want to be invited, so they stop inviting you. Before you know it, you're locked out completely and you decide to go to another smaller event.

Unless you move really far away from the stadium, you can still hear the chants and cheers from inside the walls. It's possible to move so far away from the stadium that you forget that the game is going on without you. But no matter how much you tell yourself you don't want to be a part of what's going on inside the stadium, deep down you know a part of you really does.

Giving Up

Somewhere along the way I gave up on having a relationship with my father. Convinced that lots of people had grown up fine without being close to their dads, I figured I didn't need that either. Many people grow up without the physical presence of a father. I had the physical presence, but at times I wondered if that had only made matters worse.

The thought of spending an extended period of time with Daddy by myself was scary. Even when I became an adult, with two college degrees and a successful teaching career, I still couldn't figure out what it was that set him off. I found myself getting angrier and angrier trying to understand him. Trying to change things.

I went home to my parents' during my summers off from teaching in an unconscious attempt to finally figure it out and get it right. So that maybe, after all this time, things could be right with this family—this family that had so much good about it. But I still felt disconnected from my dad.

By the time I was almost thirty years old, I had given up. I had to say, no more. He became a person I respected for providing the material things I had enjoyed, the person I respected as my father simply because I believed God called me to "honor your mother and father." Emotionally I cut him off. Every time I tried to get close to him, I got hurt all over again. I couldn't take that any more.

So I decided I would be okay without any sense of closeness to my dad. I was close to my mother. That's the way it was in some families. And that's not so bad, I'd tell myself. Lots of folks don't have either parent in their corner. I was blessed. I at least had my mother.

Just go on, Sally, I said to myself, and don't spend any more time worrying about it.

IV
The Lies Unearthed

God Goes to Paris

God can show up in the most unusual places.

Burning bushes.

Donkeys.

Carpenters.

And, for me, he showed up in a dressing room in the largest department store in Paris.

In the summer of 1991 I flew to England to spend a month with my friend, Keith, who had moved the year before to minister with a church in London. I had met Keith in the singles class at a church we were attending while he was in graduate school, and I was in my first year of teaching high school. A group of us ran around together that year, and Keith and I found ourselves enjoying each other's company beyond the weekly devotionals and volleyball games and the plethora of activities the class came up with so that no one would have to spend an evening alone. That was all well and good for some people, but to me it sometimes felt like "junior high revisited," since we were doing the same kinds of things we had done in our church youth groups.

What I enjoyed most about Keith was that we could talk about anything and everything, and we did.

Keith loved history and theology, and we had the greatest conversations about church and what we'd always believed, and how there might be a different way to look at things. Keith helped me to see that not everything is black and white. He challenged me to think. I loved that he challenged me to examine the reasons why I believed what I did. I loved that he felt comfortable coming over to my house and sitting in silence while I graded papers and sometimes helped me grade them. I loved watching TV shows with him over the phone. And I loved that he could quote lines from *The Andy Griffith Show* reruns almost as well as I could.

I liked Keith. And he liked me.

For a short while, we made a stab at dating. Once when my parents were visiting, Keith went to dinner with us, and then took us to the community theatre. He seemed nervous with my parents at dinner, and that made me nervous.

It was the strangest feeling, one that I can't describe really, but I always felt awkward being around my parents, my mother in particular, with a boy that I liked. I felt embarrassed, as though I wasn't supposed to like him. As though it would be disloyal to my mother.

That's the way I felt that night. My fear kicked in—fear of liking him and getting hurt, fear of what a real relationship with a man would look like and lead to, fear of losing myself in that relationship. After he kissed me goodnight, although it was the sweetest first kiss I'd ever experienced, I pulled away. The next morning in our Sunday school class, not only did I avoid sitting by him, I hardly spoke. And for the next several months I had no contact with him.

I look back on that time of shutting him out and feel horrible. But that's how terrified I was at the thought of having a real relationship with a man. That's how ill-equipped I was to be emotionally intimate and work through conflict with someone. I didn't know how. Worse, I was totally unaware that I didn't know. The sad thing is, Keith may have been the man I could have built a life with if I hadn't been so scared.

Somehow over the next five years we maintained a friendship in spite of my sudden, inexplicable distancing—mainly a lot of forgiveness on Keith's part—and we stayed in touch after he moved to London.

We planned my trip to visit him in the summer of 1991 so that I'd have a couple of weeks in London before touring other parts of Europe in one of those whirlwind "if it's Tuesday, it must be Switzerland" style trips through Europe. When we got to Paris, I told Keith I wanted to do some serious shopping. He took me to the largest department store—like Saks Fifth Avenue of New York or Harrods of London—the fabulous Galeries Lafayette. Keith found a chair somewhere near the dressing rooms while I gathered an assortment of outfits to try on. The store was huge, bustling, and noisy. So noisy that I hadn't even noticed the Muzak playing in the background. But when I got in the dressing room, away from the crowd, all of a sudden I heard nothing else but the voice of Natalie Cole. It was as though everything else around me had frozen in time, and the song was being played just for me.

It was the summer she cut a new album, with the title song being an old one that I was familiar with, "Unforgettable." Her father, Nat King Cole, had recorded it in the 1950s, but I'd never heard Natalie Cole sing it before. I was thinking to myself, well that's kinda sweet for her to sing a song her dad had recorded, but then I heard his voice singing with her, as though it were a duet.

"Unforgettable, that's what you are.

Unforgettable, though near or far . . . ."

Slowly the tears started coming, and I couldn't hold them back. I found myself standing in a dressing room halfway around the world, weeping uncontrollably. And I didn't know why.

I could hear this father and daughter singing a duet together—his voice dubbed because he was no longer living—and it amazed me how alike they sounded. It was as though it was the same voice, at two different octaves. As though they couldn't be separated, even by death. The words haunted me even more. No matter how hard I tried to pretend it didn't matter that I had no relationship with my father, it did matter. Very much. What would it be like to hear my father sing those words to me? To feel unforgettable to him? After all this time, facing my thirtieth birthday, there was a little girl inside me still longing for the relationship with her daddy that she'd never had. I felt the pain of that longing all alone in that dressing room.

But I wasn't alone. Even in a department store in a foreign country, my Father was right there. Not yet removing my pain, as I wished he would, but bringing it to the surface so I could really feel it. And let it guide me home.

Gay Doesn't Mean
Happy Anymore

Throughout the years I had no idea what was happening inside me. Why did I feel more comfortable in clothes our culture deemed masculine, rather than what was "girly"? Why did I feel more comfortable doing "boy" things, but was afraid to be around men? I was more comfortable around women, but I didn't feel as if I fit in with them. I wasn't "one of them." Why? How could I feel like I wanted to be male when I didn't like so many men? Women had always been the source of protection, comfort, and compassion. Men the source of danger, aloofness, and injustice.

I kept thinking that I would "grow out of it." Perhaps same-sex attraction can be a phase in some people, but that wasn't the case for me. My feelings grew stronger as I got older. By the time I realized and was able to admit, at least to myself, that I was struggling with homosexual attraction, I was twenty years old and a junior at a Christian university.

I had nowhere to ask questions, no one with whom I felt safe enough to say anything about what I was feeling. In the 1960s and 1970s, and even in the early 1980s—when the AIDS crisis finally began to wake us up—nobody talked about homosexuality except with ridicule and scorn. There were no gay characters on TV that might have at least gotten a conversation started.

There was certainly no mention at church, the place I looked to for the truth on how to view everything and on how to live.

I was scared, and I had good reason to be.

I couldn't have anything "wrong" with me. I grew up in a family where you didn't talk about your problems. Families were supposed to look like the Cleavers. If you were one of those rare, aberrant families that did have problems, you kept your dirty laundry hidden. You created the illusion of being the perfect family.

I not only belonged to the perfect family, I was also the perfect child. I simply couldn't break that bubble by admitting something was wrong—especially as "wrong" as this.

The thought of telling someone—the thought of someone finding out what I was feeling on the inside—was terrifying. Trembling, heart-pounding, take-your-breath-away terrifying.

"This isn't something you have to tell, Sally. Nobody ever has to know. Besides, they're not actions, only thoughts in your head. And they make you feel better, right?"

I listened to the voice and didn't tell a soul for another fifteen years.

Every day for the next fifteen years I asked God to take away those feelings. During those fifteen years of inward pleading and outward silence, I finished undergraduate and graduate degrees in communication, taught middle and high school speech, and coached competitive speech, debate, and theatre. I loved what I did. I loved the kids I taught. But I know I would have been a better teacher if I'd taken care of the pain and confusion that lay untouched inside of me.

But I hadn't yet reached a place where I could admit to anyone that something wasn't quite right, let alone actually begin to work through the feelings of anger, sadness, and loneliness.

I was so paralyzed by the shame and fear of anyone finding out, that I didn't have as much to give the kids as I could have.

In my conservative, small, West Texas, Bible-belt world, you truly didn't speak of such things without consequences. At the very least I feared losing my job. More important to me, though, was the fear of family never responding the same way to me again, friends walking away, being shunned at church, and never being allowed to work with kids again. As irrational as those fears might seem to some, they were all based on real-life examples. In the 1970s in Dallas, any teacher found to be gay was fired. I knew people whose friends abandoned them and talked about them behind their backs. I knew people who had been called in by church leadership and asked not to come back "until they got their lives straightened out."

I had a friend about that time whose family found out that he was living in a relationship with another man. They went to see a psychology professor at the university I attended who had the reputation of being the resident "expert" on homosexuality, seeking counsel. His advice to them, as a Christian psychologist who believed that homosexuality was contrary to God's will for a person's life, was to confront their son and demand that he move out of the house and relationship and seek help. If he chose to stay in the relationship, they should cease all communication with him until he left "that lifestyle." The sincere belief was that separation from his family would "bring him to his senses" and that he would come back home.

My friend's father asked me to come over to talk before they confronted him. He asked me all sorts of questions about his son's behavior with me, whether or not we kissed, held hands, had any sort of sexual relationship. I was embarrassed. Embarrassed for my friend. And terrified that if it was discovered that I was experiencing feelings of same-sex attraction myself that would lead to humiliation and abandonment for me as well.

His father confronted him at the Thanksgiving dinner table with his whole family present. Feeling backed into a corner, given an ultimatum to choose between this person he loved and his family, he refused to leave the relationship and his family stopped talking to him. For nearly two decades.

The thought that I might be gay scared me to death. I didn't even know to use that word because that word meant something else when I was growing up. Gay meant you were happy. Using the word "gay" or "homosexual" to describe myself was foreign to me. I didn't (and still don't) label myself as a lesbian. Those words couldn't be a part of who I was because all my life I'd believed that was more than wrong—it was probably the worst thing a person could do. Or be. I didn't believe it was okay to act on my feelings of attraction to women, but I had no idea what to do.

Restless and miserable, growing angrier at my father, I sought the help of a counselor and hoped that simply telling him about the broken relationship with my father would be enough for me to escape my misery. I couldn't bring myself to be honest about my secret. I was too ashamed. I only knew that I was miserable and had finally come to acknowledge that my recurring misery might possibly have something to do with this sexual attraction to women. Petrified of someone finding out, I kept quiet.

One of "Those"

In my world growing up, there was almost no mention of homosexuality, except to say how vile and sick it was. Or to make fun of someone, mostly men, who might exhibit what people called homosexual "tendencies."

It was no secret how the people around me felt about homosexuality. The messages were very clear.

And I knew what my mother thought, too.

One day I came home from school in the fifth grade asking what a "homo" was. A girl in my class had used that word while telling a story about insulting her younger sister. My mother explained that "homo" was an abbreviation for "homosexual" and that it was something awful—when men liked other men in a way that they were supposed to like women, or when women liked other women in a way they were only supposed to like men. She told me that she'd never heard of anything so disgusting until she was in an abnormal psychology class in college, where the professor had taught them about people who were like that, all living in New York City.

Our church held dinners featuring "womanless fashion shows" as humorous entertainment. The church leaders dressed up as women and walked down a runway, like they were in a fashion show for women's clothing. My dad was one of the men who dressed up, and my mom took pictures of all of them. Everyone laughed and thought it was hilarious. And why wouldn't they laugh? They lived in a world that watched Milton Berle dress up as a woman on TV. But if there was ever any mention of a man dressing up as a woman in a context other than for fun, that was condemned as sick and perverted.

As a kid, I didn't understand the difference so I was confused. In one place men dressing like women was funny, in another it was awful.

One Christmas my teenage cousin dressed up in a nightshirt someone had given him. He belted it, stuffed the front with balloon breasts, and came out to model for the family. Everyone laughed, thinking it was hysterical. My mother took pictures of him, too.

In a family gathering we laughed at a boy who could dress up believably as a girl, but years later, when that same boy declared himself to be gay, he was met with silence and disapproval.

The first time I ever heard anyone talk about homosexuality in reference to someone specific was when I was eight. We had gone to Carl and Tina's wedding, and I thought it was absolutely beautiful. The whole church was lighted by candles set in front of the stained glass windows that lined the walls on both sides of the auditorium. White taffeta bows adorned each pew along the aisle where the bride walked escorted by her father. Sheer elegance. Especially to an eight-year-old girl.

Carl left his wife within a few months and everyone at church was talking about it. They couldn't believe it. Because he was, as everyone said with an accompanying twist of the hand, "Well, you know, one of thooooose." How could he do that to her? How sick, I heard them say.

I picked up bits and pieces of other conversations while standing next to my mom in the foyer after church as she visited with her friends. I didn't understand all they were saying, but I understood more than they realized. I understood that whatever was the matter with Carl was horrible. They laughed nervously or curled their lips, as though they smelled something foul, and shook their heads.

Words like "perversion" and "abomination" were used in conjunction with homosexuality from the pulpit, and even though I didn't know what those words meant at the time, I knew from the preacher's tone of voice and facial expressions that it couldn't be anything good. I saw the hand gestures and the mimicry from others, sometimes within my own family.

Add a couple more decades of exposure to similar opinions and beliefs about homosexuality and I arrived at a place of utter humiliation to think that this word "gay" may, in fact, describe me.

And that's why I couldn't even begin to imagine telling anyone that I liked girls. It meant risking losing everyone I loved. Then I would have absolutely no one.

And more than anyone else, I couldn't risk losing my mother.

Miserable

After ten years of teaching, and still searching for ways to feel loved and accepted—especially by my dad—I decided to go to law school.

At the time I was deeply attracted to a dear friend who had no idea that my feelings for her went far beyond friendship. First and foremost, I was drawn to her spiritually and emotionally. We shared a bond as sisters in Christ. She loved Jesus like I did. She possessed an amazing spiritual maturity and ability to communicate on a deeply spiritual level that I had never experienced.

It's only been out of a foundation of spiritual connection and emotional intimacy that I've experienced sexual attraction to a close friend. With every close friend? No. But the emotional connection must be there first. I could never be attracted to anyone who didn't also share my deep love for God. And she had it all.

In the first semester of my second year of law school, I was wrestling with a case of endometriosis that I could no longer ignore—a painful condition that required surgery and could potentially limit my ability to have children in the future. I wasn't getting any younger, and as much as I didn't want to, I was finally coming to terms with the fact that I probably wasn't going to get married and have kids.

Between facing the possibility of not being able to have children, and the reality that I would never be able to fill the void of real intimacy in my life with relationships that only existed in my imagination, I was miserable.

Yet I knew that my decision to follow Jesus hadn't changed.

I knew God to be kind and loving and fair. And it didn't seem kind or fair for God to allow me to experience these feelings of attraction to a woman and not also be able and willing to help me in some way. I had no idea how God would help me—whether he would totally remove those feelings or whether he would empower me to live a celibate life even if I remained attracted to women. Or if I would discover that God was okay with my being in a relationship with another woman. I didn't know. I deeply wanted to discover what God wanted for my life. I wanted to know how I got where I was and how to move forward.

More than anything, I wanted to stop hurting. I'd tried everything else I knew to try to feel better and I kept ending up in the same place. Miserable. Alone. The things I'd always relied on to help me feel better—working more, achieving more, creating relationships in my head—were no longer helping.

For the first time in my life I found myself not able to hold it together, to perform above average, to be the life of the party. I could no longer live as though I had everything going for me on the outside and yet be miserably confused and full of self-doubt on the inside.

Dear God

I hated playing in my room by myself when I was a little girl. Even as a teenager I didn't hole up in my room unless I was mad. I wanted to be around people. And whether people were around or not, the TV was always on. It made me feel less alone.

I still didn't like being by myself when I started law school. But for the first time in my life I was faced with having to give my full concentration to my studies. Maybe it was because I was getting older, but I couldn't read and listen to the TV at the same time like I used to.

So I had to spend a lot of time with the TV turned off. In total silence. Weekends were the worst. I started planning days in advance so that I wouldn't find myself alone on a Saturday with nothing to do. Of course, I could've been studying, but that would surely mean being stuck in the house all by myself. And if I went to the library at the law school, I'd run into friends and end up not getting anything done.

I hated being alone.

It was toward the end of the two-week period for final exams right before the Christmas break, and I had one more exam to take before I could go home. I knew I needed to study that night but I couldn't concentrate on anything. I wanted the floor to open up and swallow me.

I had been in the same place before. A friend that I had allowed to become far more to me in my head than just a friend, not knowing the script of this romantic relationship that I had conjured up between the two of us, had not followed the script. The script called for me to be the most important person in her world, as she was in mine. When she had plans with other friends, I got my feelings hurt. When she didn't call, I was disappointed. Worse yet, when she spent time with a boyfriend, I was jealous.

If only I had kept all of those feelings to myself, but I didn't. My hurt and disappointment and jealousy came out as anger, and I was a master of making excuses for my anger, rationalizing and manipulating the circumstances to make it appear that she had been a bad friend. I could convince myself, and her, that my feelings were legitimate and that she had wronged me as a friend. But the truth was, my feelings were hurt only because she hadn't met the expectations I had contrived out of my desire to be in a romantic relationship with her. Expectations which she had no idea existed, based on feelings she couldn't possibly be expected to return.

Because she truly was a dear friend and had nothing but the best of intentions toward me as her friend, she was easily convinced that my anger was somehow her fault and she would apologize after I had gone ballistic and made her feel like a dog. And I knew the fault lay purely with me.

It had been another one of those tumultuous nights with her. But this night was different. Because I didn't feel better after that episode of ranting, then cathartic tears, followed by her apology and promise to "be a better friend" to me. On this night, not only did I not feel better, I felt worse.

How many times had this scenario played out in exactly the same fashion, with me carefully covering my tracks, making excuses, only to find myself hurt again and again because the friend—whoever it was—didn't respond in the way that I wanted her to? The definition of insanity—doing the same thing over and over, expecting a different result—flashed through my thoughts.

You're never going to have what you really want, Sally, the voice inside taunted. Even if these women had known your true feelings and returned them, you still wouldn't get what you want because you believe it's wrong to be with a woman.

You expected to be in a different place when you got to be in your thirties, didn't you, Sally? You expected all this confusion and fear would disappear and that you'd find some guy to marry and have a family. But that hasn't happened the way you thought it would, has it? And now you're going to have surgery for this endometriosis next month, and every doctor you've talked to says it almost always comes back. You've really screwed up your life, haven't you?

I curled up on the love seat, trying to comfort myself with another bowl of Blue Bell ice cream and chocolate syrup. I tried to distract myself with TV. But nothing stopped the tears. Tears of regret, shame, fear, and confusion. I had no earthly clue as to how to help myself. And absolutely no one to talk to. Like the psalmist, I too cried out to the Lord:

> I pour out my complaints before him,
>> I tell him all my troubles.
> When I am overwhelmed,
>> You alone know the way I should turn.
> Wherever I go,
>> My enemies have set traps for me.
> I look for someone to come and help me,
>> But no one gives me a passing thought!
> No one will help me;

No one cares a bit what happens to me.
Then I pray to you, O Lord.
    I say, "You are my place of refuge.
    You are all I really want in life.
Hear my cry,
    For I am very low.
Rescue me from my persecutors,
    For they are too strong for me.
Bring me out of prison
    So I can thank you.
The godly will crowd around me,
    For you are good to me."

PSALM 142, NLT

For a long time that night, into the wee hours of the next morning, I wept. Instead of studying for the law school exam, I decided to pour my heart out to God in a letter. I still didn't have the courage even to say the word "homosexual" out loud, especially if it was in reference to myself, but I believed at the time that it would be enough just to say it in the letter.

Using pink paper and red roller ball ink, I began to write.

Lord, I didn't think this would matter because it's just been in my head. You know, like Dr. Brecheen said in Bible class that one day when somebody asked the question about when homosexuality became a sin, and he said it wasn't wrong until you acted on it. I thought as long as I didn't act on it, it was okay. I didn't have to tell anybody or do anything about it as long as I didn't act on it. As long as I didn't have sex with anybody, it'd be okay. So I didn't. Wasn't that enough?

I should have known better, because you said, "as a man thinks in his heart, so is he." I guess that applies to women, too.

I'm in the same place I was in when I finally realized that I was never going to have what I wanted with Renee. Now here it is six years later and I'm back again—realizing that I've done the same thing all over again with someone else. I don't want these feelings. I've been telling you that and asking you to take them away for over a decade. Every single day, some days more than others, and yet I'm still here, with those feelings growing deeper and stronger for women I could never have because they don't love me in the same way I love them, and never would. And even if they did, I don't believe that's okay. I have no idea what I'm supposed to do with all this.

Really, all I did was play a game in my head—I let my feelings for a friend go beyond friendship, but only in my head. Just like planning those trips with Papa when I was little, just like imagining trips to Six Flags with Kenneth in junior high, knowing all the time that it wasn't real, but they made me feel better at the time. Like I wasn't completely alone. Like I had somebody to be with me, you know? Like I had that one person in my life who mattered most, and to whom I mattered most. The person you're supposed to share everything with, who knows more about you than anyone, and loves you all the more. That's all I wanted.

All I did was pretend that this girl who is my dearest friend was really more than a friend. It made me feel less alone. Only now it's become more difficult. Because she has no idea how I really feel about her. She thinks of me only as a friend—a close friend, yes, a friend who loves me, yes, but not like that. Not like I care for her. And so I know she's doing what she's supposed to do—she has other friends, and she has this boyfriend whom she's growing closer to all the time. She's not supposed to just be with me, but that's what I'd like. I feel so jealous when it's obvious that someone else comes first with her. It makes me feel left out, forgotten, all alone again.

She doesn't know how I feel and I can't possibly tell her. She wouldn't have anything to do with me then, for sure. I can't tell anyone. No one would want anything to do with me if they knew. It's hard enough admitting it to you, but maybe that's what I need to do. Maybe I'll feel better if I confess it to you. If I tell you that I think what I'm struggling with is—oh God, I can't even say it out loud. Surely not, surely I'm not homosexual.

It feels like it did when I liked Kenneth when we were kids or when I liked Eddie in college, but it goes way beyond those feelings. More intimate. I don't think you made me this way, but I don't know how I got here. I'm miserable where I am. I can't stand this roller coaster I'm on. I feel wonderful when I'm with her and things are good between us, but I'm miserable the minute she does something that hurts my feelings. And I know that it's only a matter of time before she marries that boy and I can't stand the thought of that. She has no idea and I'm not supposed to have these feelings for her anyway, but I do, and God, oh dear God, I don't know what to do about that. Oh please, don't make me tell someone—everyone will find out and my life will be over. I'll be alone forever.

All this time I gave you other parts of me, parts of me that were easy to give, but I held this one back. I held onto it because I found something that made me feel less alone, like nothing else did and I wanted to hang onto it. I still do. But I'm so miserable right now that I'll give you this part of me, too. Only because I believe you do still love me. I believe you're a just God. I don't believe you would tell me not to do something and then not provide any way of helping me, especially when it feels so right for me. I don't know how you'll do that. I don't know whether you'll change me so that I want to be with a man. I can't fathom that right now, because the only person I care about being with is her.

I'm sick to my gut of being alone. But I'm petrified of being in a relationship—with anybody. Not that anybody would want me in the first place. Even if they did, I don't know how to be in a relationship—a real relationship—with anyone. I don't know why I can't figure this out—why everyone else seems to be able to do this and I can't—and I don't even know where to begin to learn. I don't know who to trust to talk to about any of this. But maybe that's what you want me to do?

I read the letter over once, and then for fear of something happening before I could dispose of it and someone finding it, for fear of someone discovering that Sally Gary, the good little Church of Christ girl was homosexual, I tore the letter into the tiniest pieces I could muster and carried them very carefully in a sack through the darkness to the dumpster in the parking lot. As though I were ridding myself of the murder weapon after dumping the body, I looked around to make sure it was safe, that no one could have seen me dump the pieces, and then I scattered them in different parts of the dumpster.

I didn't sleep that entire night. The next morning I was in no shape to take an exam, so I called the law school and asked if I could reschedule.

As exhausted as I was from no sleep and the emotional turmoil, there was a peace at that moment. Even though my greatest fear was about to be exposed. Because I could hear God saying to me, in a voice that was ever so kind, ever so still, "Tell somebody, honey. I don't want you to walk through this by yourself. Not anymore."

Listening with the Heart

I called and made an appointment with the counselor I'd gone to during the last year of teaching high school about my relationship with my father. The counselor who had absolutely no idea what I'd been keeping from him.

I had chosen the counselor carefully. He had worked on some research and writing projects with my favorite professor from college. I knew he had the credentials in psychology, he was a Christian, and my favorite professor trusted him. I thought maybe I could trust him, too. But I didn't know how he would react. He might react with the same facial expressions I had seen on preachers' faces from the pulpit, looks of disgust, as though they couldn't stand the thought of being near someone "like that." He might not want to deal with me and refer me to someone else.

I had to take the chance. I had to tell someone.

On a bitter cold, snowy day, with ice on the roads and a small voice telling me to run the car off the side of the road and no one would be the wiser, I drove three hours to his office in north Dallas. My heart pounded as I approached the door, praying I wouldn't see anyone I knew as I walked into the waiting room.

As I pushed open the door and entered the waiting room, the first person I saw was a guy I had gone to college with and hadn't seen in fifteen years. He looked up from the magazine he was reading and smiled. Then looked away, probably as embarrassed at being seen there as I was. Then I turned to the receptionist and couldn't believe it. There sat the former youth minister's wife from my home church twenty-five years before, the woman who had stood with me as I dried off after my baptism saying over and over, "Oh, sweet girl. Oh, sweet girl." Just as she greeted me, her husband, now one of the psychologists in the office, walked in. I was scared half to death. These people had known and loved me since I was a little girl. Would they still love me if they knew?

My paranoia also told me I had a label that instantly exposed me to everyone in the room. As though, like Hester Prynne's scarlet letter "A," I wore an "H" for homosexual emblazoned on my chest. If anyone found out that I was seeking a counselor to talk about an attraction to my own gender, oh my. What would they think?

I remember a lot of things about that day—the day I first told someone I liked girls. I remember the office we were in and where I was sitting. I remember what I was wearing. But I don't remember what he said to me in response to my declaration. In fact, I don't think he said much of anything. Mostly he just listened. The expression on his face never changed. His countenance never grew cold or resistant. He remained warm and inviting, as though nothing I said shocked him. As though he felt no revulsion toward me at all.

Scary as it was, I felt a great sense of freedom in finally telling someone. Nothing instantly changed inside me. I still had no idea what to do with all those feelings. But at least now it wasn't my own secret.

We talked for a couple of hours that morning, and not only did he not walk away, he invited me to come back for a couple more hours that afternoon. Although I was relieved to be welcomed back, I couldn't help but wonder if that meant that I was really screwed up!

It did.

And I am.

But no more than all the rest of us.

That happened over sixteen years ago and since that time I've had the opportunity to share that secret of mine with thousands of people all over the world. I wouldn't have had the courage to do that if I hadn't found a safe place to pour my heart out that very first time. What would've happened if he had not responded so warmly? What if the gentle smile and the kindness of his eyes had been replaced by a wrinkled brow and no smile? Or worse yet, what if he hadn't looked at me at all?

I don't think he knew all the answers at that moment. But what he did know is that having all the answers as to how to "fix" me wasn't what I needed. He knew it was more important to listen. If nothing else, to be willing to absorb some of the agonizing pain of carrying an unbearable secret for most of my life. Most importantly, he knew Jesus. He knew how to look at me through the eyes of Christ, to listen with the Good Shepherd's heart of compassion, and to extend the same hospitality to me that he himself had received. Never once did he tell me what he thought about homosexuality. Never once did he quote Scripture to me in that first meeting. In the weeks and months and years ahead, we never ever looked at the passages in Genesis or Leviticus or Romans or 1 Corinthians or 1 Timothy. Because I knew they were there. And he was wise enough to meet me where I hurt, just as Jesus did for all those he encountered.

When I left the office that day I didn't have any answers. He didn't give me any assignments. I wasn't given any books to read. In a way it would've been nice to have those things, because that was the way part of me has been wired—to think my way out of difficulties, to find a rational, academic solution to the problem, to critically analyze and outline the answer to the question. But that wasn't what I needed right then—if ever.

What I needed was to tell someone who would listen. With his heart.

Little Girl

Having admitted to myself and to the counselor that I experienced same-sex attraction, I thought all of our conversation was going to be centered around sex. I thought that all we'd talk about was how I felt about girls—I thought we'd talk about the very few girls I'd been attracted to and what my relationships with them had been like. Much to my surprise, that's not what we talked about at all.

We talked about what life had been like for me as a little girl.

We talked about what the little girl who was inside me had grown up believing about herself.

We talked about how she felt.

How afraid she was.

How hurt she was.

How angry she was.

And how confused she was as to what it meant to be feminine.

Not just confused, but ashamed.

It took a long time for all of this talk about "what my little girl felt" to make sense to me—really, to get to a point that I didn't roll my eyes every time the counselor started talking about my "little girl." For the longest time I thought all his talk was a bunch of psycho-mumbo-jumbo that made no sense. I couldn't see what all this talk about how I saw myself and my relationship with my dad could possibly have anything to do with my current feelings of sexual attraction to women.

The visits felt like a waste of time and money. Flying from Lubbock to Dallas once a week, while I was in the middle of law school, costing me not only airfare and cab fare, but a mounting bill that I would owe him when I finished. Whenever that would be. And how was I supposed to know? How would I know when I was "better"?

Week after week the stories that surfaced, the feelings that bubbled up from those conversations, often left me feeling worse when I left his office. I felt stupid doing the things he asked me to do to "find my little girl," like taking bubble baths or going to the park to swing on the swing set. I was supposed to go to Sonic for a vanilla Dr Pepper in the middle of the day or to the Dairy Queen for an ice cream cone. Things that the little girl in me loved to do, but rarely, if ever, got to do in the hectic pace of my adult life.

I carried out my assignments alone. After all, who would understand? In my generation, the stigma of going to a counselor was bad enough, but if they knew what he was asking me to do? Oh my! I'd surely be declared a nut case.

In the midst of the pain and embarrassment that stemmed from the rational, logical side that dominated most of my being, something amazing began to happen. While retelling and re-experiencing those events and revisiting all those beliefs about myself and the world around me brought a tremendous amount of pain, it also brought an incredible amount of freedom and release. For the first time in my life the little girl in me began to feel safe to express the pain she never got to express as a child. For the first time she was able to feel and give voice to the hurt and frustration and anger she often felt growing up. Just as reopening an infected wound to release the accumulated pus is the only way to heal the physical body, re-examining the emotional wounds of my past was one of the ways God used to heal this little girl's heart.

Telling My Parents

A long while passed before I told anyone else that I was attracted to girls. After that December day in the counselor's office, the next person I told was my mother, the Saturday before Mother's Day. She had come to visit me without Daddy because, at the counselor's recommendation, I requested he not come, and they honored that.

She sat on one end of an oblong ottoman in my living room. I was so afraid to tell her, so ashamed, that rather than sitting directly in front of her on the chair, I sat on the opposite end of the ottoman. I couldn't bear to look her in the eyes and see her disappointment.

Slowly, hesitantly, I told her that yes, I was going to see the counselor about Daddy as I had told them before, but even more so, it was because I was attracted to girls. It didn't come out as smooth as all that, and I don't remember exactly what I said, but I do know that as we talked, I could sense nothing in her tone that reflected any sort of change toward me.

The only question from her was a question I've heard from many people since then, as though the sexual behavior is the single most important aspect of someone feeling different in regard to their sexuality. She said, "You haven't done anything with anyone have you?" I was heartbroken to think that after all this time, her love really was conditional—that she might only love me as long as I hadn't acted on my sexual feelings of attraction. As though this part of me that felt so core to who I was merely involved sexual behavior.

I was fearful of Daddy's reaction, that he would become angry at me, feeling, like so many parents do, that I was placing the blame on him. I feared it would trigger another fit of rage. He did become angry when Mama told him, then he wept. He began to blame himself and became extremely regretful and sorrowful. Even now he continues to apologize for not knowing how to be a father to me or how to be a good husband to my mother.

To my parents' credit, after my revelation they never changed the way they related to me. Certainly they went through a range of emotions that I think most parents go through upon hearing that a son or daughter is gay—from sadness, to guilt, to defensive anger. Many times they avoided the conversation because they didn't know what to say. Other times, my mother in particular, minimized it as though there was nothing to talk about. As though I hadn't really said I was attracted to women. But one of the greatest blessings of my life is that my parents never turned away. Even further, the most remarkable gift is that my parents entered into this process of discovery with me.

We made lots of trips to Dallas for counseling. From the beginning we all three realized this journey wasn't about "fixing" Sally or about "tending to Sally's problem." This wasn't about "Sally being gay," this was about a family system that needed help in moving toward what God had intended.

I'm so thankful for their participation in the process; it's been much easier that way. It's been a family trip, exploring a system of interacting with each other in ways that were never what God intended—and allowing him to reteach us how to be a family. I can't imagine having to do this alone, without them. Together we came to see that acknowledging the truth—the truth that unhealthy patterns of relating to one another had impacted my development in many ways—didn't take away from all the good that existed in this family. I'm so thankful that, rather than allowing shame and guilt to cripple them from exploring this with me, or letting defensive pride keep them from learning things about themselves and their own relationship, they entered into this wholeheartedly. It was grueling and uncomfortable at times, especially at first. It was difficult financially and emotionally, but we couldn't have spent that time doing anything more important.

My dad learned how much I needed his presence and affirmation. After a long while, I learned that I had developed a completely understandable, but inappropriate over-attachment to my mother. An over-dependence that prevented me from maturing emotionally in a way that allowed me to grow into a full sense of myself as a woman. And this shaped my picture of self and my views of men and women and relationships as much as any experience with my father ever did. My mom listened and tried to understand what it was I needed—for her to let go. It wasn't that I didn't need her anymore, because I did. I do. Rather, I needed our mother/daughter roles to evolve into the adult relationship God designed for parent and child to grow into.

Sometimes it's hard to realize that so much good could come from such a broken family system. Growing up in the 1960s you learned that you didn't talk about anything that went on in your family that didn't look like the Cleavers. But the truth was, there were things that happened in my family that never should've happened. Things that God never intended for his children to experience. Truth is, those moments shaped me. It's a difficult process, the sorting through the mix of wonderful moments and painful events, the words that damaged and the words that empowered, and to realize that they came from the same source. I think we had believed that if we admitted the bad, it would negate all the good that took place.

Recounting the hurtful events of our past served to demonstrate God's great power not only to sustain us but to heal our hearts and the relationships. Unless I tell you how bad it was, you can't fully know how good God is to restore and to redeem lives that the enemy meant to destroy. If I sugarcoated it—if I pretend that we lived like the Cleavers—you'd never know how amazing this God of ours is.

And because of my parents' hearts being so open to change, I learned how much each of them really did love me.

Are we all fixed now? Hardly. Are we better than we were? Most definitely.

V
Living in the Tension

Real Friends

It was another cold day. Another long drive. But this time the drive was to see someone I loved. A friend I trusted with the deepest, darkest secrets of my life. Somehow I knew that what I had to tell Darlene wouldn't change anything between us. Crazy as it was, I knew she would understand and love me all the more. Most of all, I knew she would keep my eyes fixed on Jesus.

I got up early so I could be there in time for lunch. A skinny hazelnut latte from Starbucks and the economy sized bag of Hot Tamales candy from Sam's kept me alert and focused on the road. In some ways the trip was similar to the one I'd made awhile back, a confessional journey, but this time I didn't need the words of "Breath of Heaven" to keep me on the road. I had every desire to stay on the road, knowing that my God never wavered in his love for me. His delight in me. I believed in that love to the core of my soul.

That's why this trip was different.

This time I didn't tremble with fear. This time the thought of confession didn't make my stomach turn, for fear that my relationship with this friend would never be the same. But I knew I needed a safe place to share the deepest places of my heart.

I'd learned a better way to live, in openness and honesty with those closest to me, and I knew I didn't have to live in secrecy anymore. That's where the lies grow until you can't discern what's true and what's not. Lies look more like truth when kept in the dark of secrecy. It's hard to discern the truth all alone. It's hard to figure out which path to follow when you feel as if you have to keep everything to yourself.

I don't know what I'd do without those safe places that I have found in a handful of close friends. Friends who love me unconditionally and love Jesus like I do. Friends who listen and pray and stay connected to me. No matter what.

We met at a restaurant. From the moment she got out of the car and hugged me I felt safe. She wasn't in any hurry to let go of me. She never is. She's been one of those friends who knows that there's nothing about hugging me that "turns me on" or causes me to feel the least bit attracted to her. I've never been physically attracted to this friend, even though I feel a deep spiritual and emotional connection to her, and have from the moment we became friends. Often she'll tease me about never having been attracted to her—"What am I, chopped liver?" she'll say, and we'll laugh. Being able to joke with her like that is such a gift.

We caught up with small talk as we ordered our lunch. Then I figured we didn't have much time, so I got right to the point. I told her that I had crossed a line that I thought I'd never cross with another woman. And instead of feeling remorse in that moment, I found the experience to feel completely natural. But I felt deeply conflicted as to how I could have gone from being convinced that was wrong on one day, and utterly confused by the questions I now had about resolving faith and homosexuality in the next.

We kept eating. She looked across the table at me with the sweetest expression of pain for my confusion, and compassion that reassured me she wasn't going anywhere.

"Why don't you spend the night with us? We'll pick up the kids from school, fix supper, and then you can go to church with us. You can go home tomorrow. How does that sound?"

It was a Wednesday.

"Sure, but I didn't bring anything to spend the night."

"Whatever we don't have you can get by without for one night."

So we kept talking. She listened as I explained my physical attraction to a woman has always grown out of a deep spiritual and emotional connection, beginning with a common love for God and a sweet friendship that developed out of that. All the ideas that people express about the sexual pervertedness of homosexuality, the promiscuity, the idea that homosexuality is purely about the sexual act, didn't hold true for me. That wasn't at all the way this had played out for me.

I believe God intended sex to be a celebration of the emotional connection that develops between two people, and that's precisely what this felt like. Everything about that relationship becoming sexual felt very right to me. And yet the sexual expression of my love for and commitment to this woman went against everything I had been raised to believe was right.

The tears came as I said, "This is what our brothers and sisters have been wrestling with alone and in silence. We don't feel safe to process those feelings because we've heard such hurtful things in church. How can we admit to a silent or angry church what we're feeling and be allowed to question anything?"

By this time my friend was crying too. "You know, there's a part of me that wants to tell you to go and live your life and be happy."

Of course a big part of me wanted to hear that. But another big part of me also still believed that living in a relationship with another woman wasn't right.

"I don't believe it's what God intended," she went on, "but there's an awful lot I don't understand. I don't know that anybody fully understands homosexuality."

What I wanted was for her to have all the answers, to say, "Okay, Sally, here's what you do . . . ." But I was thankful that she was willing to say she didn't have it all figured out either.

We finished lunch, and continued to talk on the drive to Walmart and I confessed my inability to always remain kind, gentle, and patient when people in the store got in our way, moving like massive icebergs, taking hours to find the right jar of pickles. After all, being unkind and impatient wasn't God's intent for me either.

In the midst of figuring out what we needed for supper, I continued to talk, and my friend listened, stopping when she felt something needed her undivided attention.

Like my questions about Scripture.

"I don't believe homosexuality is wrong because of a few passages of Scripture," I told her. "If it's wrong, it has to be for a bigger reason than 'it says so in Romans 1.' People have so many different thoughts about interpreting Scripture—even about the reliability of Scripture through all of its translations. If it's not God's intent, then it has to be for a bigger, clearer reason."

We put our conversation on hold when we went to pick up the kids from school. We prepared dinner in the kitchen as the kids told us about their day and did their homework. In a way, I couldn't believe what was taking place in that moment. That I could have shared what I had over lunch and still be with her hours later, participating in her family as though I'd told her about something as innocuous as my first day at a new job. That I could still be here, simply living life with my friend as I always had, interacting with her children as I always had, getting ready to share a meal and go to Wednesday night church with her and her family as I always had.

The fact that she didn't reject me spoke volumes. And it kept me right where I needed to be. Open. Honest. Vulnerable. Receptive.

Later that night, after dinner, church, and putting her children to bed, we picked up the conversation where we left off.

My friend curled up on one end of the sofa, tucking her toes underneath a fleece throw. "The interpretation questions, the translation questions are tricky, aren't they? There are so many schools of belief. And I think we all sort of view Scripture through filters, with some of us viewing everything, say, through the words of Jesus. Anything that doesn't match up with the way Jesus would've responded, then, becomes less important."

"Many people filter their view of theology or Scripture through the words of their pastor or some famous Bible teacher."

"Exactly. And some people view the words of Paul with more authority, so they run everything through that filter. The filter approach opens us up to conflicting views of Scripture, but can make for more interesting dialogue when people are willing to patiently engage with each other, to really listen to the other's perspective."

I pushed off my shoes with my toes. "There's the argument that because Jesus didn't say anything specifically about homosexuality that it must not be that important to him."

"He said quite a bit, though, about sexuality in general," my friend said, challenging me. "Any time a sexual relationship is presented in the Gospels—anywhere in Scripture, for that matter—it's always in the context of a committed relationship between a man and a woman."

About that time her husband came in with a cup of tea for each of us—something he's always done that amazes me. First, because he likes drinking hot tea, and second, that the guy prepares it and brings it to us without us even asking. Every time he hands me my cup, I ask him if he has a brother . . . .

He sat across from the sofa in a big, leather easy chair.

My friend sipped her tea. She cupped the mug with her hands and continued. "Scripture was meant to be viewed in its entirety, as a love story between God and people, centuries of people, so some of it is written in ways that were more relevant to the generation it was written in. That's not to say that there isn't application for us as well, but some parts, the listing of genealogies, for instance, were included to appeal to an ancient Jewish audience that deeply valued lineage. The list itself might be boring to us today, but it served its purpose for a particular audience."

"So are you saying that some things don't apply to us today?"

"Some things might be more culturally bound, like women covering their heads, for instance, but then we go back to the question of deciding what parts we're to take literally and which parts serve us more figuratively. That's what becomes difficult."

"No kidding. What I've always come back to is the challenge of surrendering every part of myself to God. That's what I decided initially, that I was holding back this one part of myself, my sexuality, from God's purview. And yet I believe that being a follower of Jesus means that everything about me is given over to God, to transform me more and more into the likeness of Christ. I find myself still asking how this impacts my sexuality."

My listening friends nodded.

"I thought I had this all figured out when I was younger. It seems the older I get, the more I realize I don't have all the answers I thought I did."

Her husband chuckled. "Join the club! I think that's where God wants us. In the tension of all those questions, not having all the answers, searching desperately to find our way, when we finally come to the place where we realize we can't do this on our own or figure out all the answers—and we have to rely on him, and him alone, to live as he calls us."

"But what if he really doesn't care about this? What if I spend my whole life by myself, because I believe that's what God wanted me to do, only to find out that I didn't have to? I mean, isn't it possible that I could live a life that's pleasing to God in a committed, monogamous relationship with another woman—a woman who also loves God—and together we find ways to serve God and further the kingdom through that relationship? What would be so wrong with that? We're not talking about a sexually promiscuous lifestyle, outside of a loving relationship—I'm talking about a spiritually, emotionally intimate relationship built on selfless love and commitment. What does it matter if that's between two men or two women?"

I didn't ask my questions out of rebelliousness, but out of the deepest desire for connection to another human being. Because after all, God's design was not for us to be alone. God created us to be in relationship. No matter how we got where we are, that desire—that need for intimacy and connection with another person—still needs to be filled. And understanding many of the reasons I experience same-sex attraction didn't fill that need for relationship. In many ways, it made me more keenly aware of what I was missing.

"I'm tired of being alone." The tears flowed down my cheeks.

Darlene came and sat next to me with her arm around me and Bill reached over and put his hand on my knee while I cried.

"That's the part that bothers me most about this struggle," he said, "knowing how alone you feel. Any time you don't want to be alone you always have a place with us."

"That's really sweet," I answered, wiping my nose with the napkin he'd given me. "I know I can come and be with you guys any time. There are lots of couples and families at church that I can go sit with, too. I can go to dinner with them or go hang out at their homes, but the fact is, no matter how wonderful a time I may have with them, I still go home by myself. Do you know how many times I've walked out of a Sunday morning service, feeling absolutely wonderful, feeling loved by so many people, but by the time I get to the car, I realize that I'm all by myself?"

I took a deep breath. "Sometimes that's fine—sometimes that's what I prefer—but the truth is, there are a lot of times that I miss having someone to simply share my life with. Someone who knows me in ways that only somebody you live with and cook with and argue with and make plans for the future with knows you. Someone who knows all the quirks of your extended family at holidays. Someone who goes to sleep with you at night and wakes up with you in the morning. And yeah, I know a lot of people don't have that, for a lot of different reasons. But there's a deep pain to this, knowing that you could never have that in a way that feels most natural to you, and still have the acceptance of your family, of your church family, and maybe even some people might think, of God."

"What that says to me is that we as a church have to be better about responding to the loneliness, especially," Bill said.

"God adores you, Sally," Darlene said. "He delights in you just as you are, right in this moment of questioning, struggling. I think if God knows the number of hairs on our heads that means he also cares about the intricate details of our lives. I think he cares about every part of you. He especially cares about how you see and value yourself."

We continued to talk into the wee hours of the morning. I didn't have any more answers at the end of that conversation than I did before it began, but I felt better. I felt better just having a place to sort through all that I was thinking and feeling, in the safety of a friendship in the Body of Christ.

That wasn't the last conversation we had. I've had hundreds of conversations over the years. With those friends. With others, whom God has equipped to help me sort through my questions. Questions that our brothers and sisters who grew up going to church, who love God and want to serve him, and yet find themselves deeply attracted to their own gender have asked and wrestled with for a lifetime. Questions about whether or not these feelings define us. Questions about the morality of homosexuality and the ability of Scripture to answer those questions. Questions about the authority of Scripture, and how to interpret the rare passages that pertain to homosexuality specifically. Questions about how God really feels about homosexuality. Questions about the very nature of God himself. And in my darkest moments, still crying out to God, I even wondered if he really did exist.

And very selfishly I asked, "Why me? Why is it that I have to struggle with this? Why won't you take those feelings away if you really don't want me to act on them?"

I keep talking to God. Talking and crying and screaming at times, with irreverence that would make Anne Lamott seem pious. But what I've learned is that my God is big enough to handle me and all my emotions. All my questions. Big enough, powerful enough to stay with me through the tension.

That's where I find myself living a lot of times, in the tension of this struggle. It's torturous at times not to have clear-cut answers. But my inability to understand, to explain, to know for certain makes me all the more dependent on the grace of God.

I don't know what I would've done if my friend had given me an ultimatum that day. Or if the handful of friends who walk beside me, who know the daily struggle this is for me at times, put time limits on my periods of frustration and doubt. If they suddenly decided one day that my mistakes were too egregious, my sin too overwhelming. What has been most helpful to me in the last fifteen years is having people around me who allow me to question, to ponder, to not have to decide everything in a moment, trusting God to work in my life in his timing.

All that God asks, I believe, is that I keep crying out to him. That I stay connected to him. That I get up every morning and get down on my knees giving every part of myself up to him, asking him to change each part that doesn't fit what he wants for me, and recognizing that I can't begin to do that alone. Only by the grace of God and the power of the Holy Spirit who resides in me as a believer in Christ Jesus can I begin to live the life God wants for me.

I don't know how to do this apart from the Body of Christ. My brothers and sisters who get what a difficult journey this is also remind me that there are other journeys that are equally, if not more difficult. They don't minimize my journey or treat me as though I need to "just get over it." My closest friends let me think aloud without always having to challenge what I say. Without facial expressions that show disapproval or disappointment or fear. They trust God to provide what I need. Most of all, they trust my love for God.

How blessed I am to have people in my life who love me like our Father. Unconditionally.

A New Daddy

I've heard it said that when it feels like you have reached the end of a relationship, you go back to the beginning. At least that's what you do if it's a relationship you want to hold on to. I think that's what I did with my dad.

Taking care of my "little girl" and learning what she needed led me to attempt to do things with my daddy. Things I'd always wanted to do. With heart pounding I began to make small plans. Tiny steps toward him, hoping to finally close the distance between us.

One year for his birthday I gave him tickets to the circus. It was awkward and I felt stupid giving them to him because I didn't know how he'd respond. But when he grinned as he read the tickets and said he'd go, the little girl inside of me was thrilled. And she was even more thrilled sitting there eating cotton candy and popcorn with her daddy while the two of them watched the tigers jump through hoops.

Once I gave him a baseball and two baseball gloves and we played catch in the backyard like we did when I was little. It was the first time it didn't hurt my hand to catch one of his hard throws.

By the time I was in college I hated football—all sports really—because I felt as if sports meant more to my dad than I did. My father can remember scores and plays from small-town high school and college football games, players' histories and records, far better than he knows the details of my life. Or so I believed. As a little girl I tried to learn everything I could about the sports he liked, basketball and football, in particular, but my knowledge didn't seem to matter, so I gave up.

One of the things I found myself wanting to do as the Lord repaired my relationship with my dad was to reconnect with him through sports. I found myself actually wanting to watch the Dallas Cowboys play on Sunday afternoons—and I didn't care that they lost most of the time! My dad started calling me at halftime and we'd talk about the game. I was relearning all the rules I had forgotten over the years, and some new ones I'd never known. And in the process, building a sweet connection with the daddy I so longed for growing up. One year I gave him tickets to the Cowboys' season opener and we watched them win the game against the brand new Houston Texans, which was almost as miraculous as this father and daughter eating hotdogs together in the stands.

Growing up, my father's hugs were awkward gestures where he'd put his arms around my shoulders, give a quick squeeze, and then place his hands on my shoulders and literally push me away. I was in my mid-forties before I was able to tell him not to hug me like that anymore. He listened, understood, and has never let go of me first again.

If you had told me when I was a little girl—or even when I was a young adult—that someday I would have a relationship with my father in which I was free to tell him anything, I would've smiled politely and said, "Well, that would be nice." Inwardly I would've felt a mixture of anger and sadness that you would even suggest such a thing, because, you see, you don't know my dad.

I wouldn't have believed that someday my daddy would call me on the telephone, on his own, just to talk to me. Before then we'd never had a phone conversation between just the two of us. When I was in college and my roommates' fathers called them, I was fascinated. I didn't mean to eavesdrop on their conversations, but I so longed to have that kind of communication with my own father, that I listened, hoping to figure out how it was done. My father had never picked up the phone and called me; he'd always left that up to my mom. So to have my father call me on the phone, without my mom, was huge.

So it was amazing that we would have wonderful conversations about how to use a Mac computer, or how bad the Cowboys played, or how well my high school band marched on the field at the game the last weekend. And that the little girl in me would've felt perfectly safe and at ease to do that with her daddy.

Or that every year on my spiritual birthday—the day I was baptized—my daddy would never fail to call me and say, "I just called to tell you happy birthday."

When the *Harry Potter* books came out, I bought two copies and gave one set to my dad and asked him to read them with me. We'd read a chapter and then talk about it on the phone. When the first movie came out, we went to see it together. And yes, we ate popcorn.

There's a scene in the first *Harry Potter* book that captured my heart from the first time I read it. Harry finds the Mirror of Erised in an abandoned wing of the Hogwarts' school and is captivated by the image he discovers when he stands in front of the life-sized mirror. Harry always sees himself as a boy with his mother and father smiling and happy. Professor Dumbledore explains to him that anyone who looks in the mirror sees the deepest desire of his heart, and since Harry's been orphaned since infancy, his deepest desire is to be reunited with his parents.

In many ways that's what my current relationship with my father feels like, as though I had been given the opportunity to have what my heart has desired since I was a little girl. Not just to imagine what it would be like, but to live it out in actual relationship with my dad.

Amazing what God can do.

The sweetest moments of all have been the conversations we've had about the stories I've written in this book—some of the things that happened in the past that we'd never spoken about, like the Christmas when I was a sophomore in high school. To be able to have those conversations with my dad, with both of my parents, about their recollection of events—to be able to ask Daddy what he was thinking, feeling, going through in those moments—to find out what it was like for him as well, has been as healing as anything I've ever experienced.

To hear my father say, "You tell the truth, Sally, tell what really happened," tells you everything you need to know about my daddy. He's as honest as the day is long. He's not perfect, and if you're thinking that my family is all "fixed" now, and that I'm all "fixed," you'd be sadly mistaken. The difference is in our ability to communicate, to talk through feelings and discuss things that happen, to bring everything into the light where the enemy has no power—that's what healing looks like for us. Not perfection, but a connection and commitment to each other, depending on God to see us through. We won't be perfect until Jesus comes to get us—and just like my mama sang, we shall see the King someday.

Lies Uprooted

The father of lies accomplishes most of his purposes in us by lying to us. About ourselves. About each other. About God. About everything. Sadly, he starts feeding us those lies before we are even capable of comprehending that they're lies. We're raised within family systems filled with people who have also bought into lies, so their lies are sometimes passed on as truth. And before we know it, we're grown adults living lives that are based on many lies, and we don't even realize it.

I can only speak for me, but I believe much of my attraction to women grew out of lies that I was conditioned to believe all my life. From the very beginning. Before I even knew what was happening.

I believed that men were scary and unpredictable.

I believed that men were thoughtless and uncaring.

I believed that men were stupid.

I believed that women were consistent, loving, and kind. A constant source of comfort.

I believed that relationships between men and women were only necessary to perpetuate the species and because men were incompetent to care for themselves.

I believed that men basically tolerated women for housekeeping, cooking, and sex. And for caring for the children they really didn't want in the first place.

I believed that the men I knew from church who appeared to be good and kind when I saw them with their wives and children were probably the same as my father when they were at home.

I believed the families I saw on TV weren't real. Fathers couldn't ever be like Andy Taylor or John Walton or Cliff Huxtable, as much as I might wish they could.

I believed that my father didn't like me. Not only did he not like me, he didn't even love me. I believed my father didn't like me because I was a girl. I believed he would've liked me more had I been a boy.

I believed I wasn't pretty.

I believed I wasn't very smart.

I believed I wasn't good at anything.

I believed I didn't fit in with the other kids. Unless I could make them laugh.

I believed I was always on the fringe with other girls. I fit, but I didn't fit. When I was around them, I was often included, but I didn't believe any of them would ever want me for their best friend.

I believed I couldn't do a lot of things that women were supposed to do—take care of babies, cook, sing.

I believed that I wasn't desirable as a girl.

I believed it would've been better for me to be a boy.

Boys could protect themselves.

People were more interested in the things boys did.

Boys got to be the leaders of everything.

If I were a boy, I would've fit into my family more. I could've protected my mother.

I could've been a preacher and married a sweet girl who loved God like I did. And life would've been a whole lot easier.

The sad thing is that none of those things that I sincerely believed growing up are true. Every single one of them is a lie. From the time I was a little girl, those lies started forming in my head and taking root in my heart, shaping how I saw myself, how I saw the roles of men and women, the worth and value of masculinity and femininity. Those lies shaped how I saw marriage and the desirability of that kind of relationship in my life, and my ability to live that out as a woman.

Certainly if I hadn't grown up believing any of those lies, my life would've been much different. But even if only a few of them had been removed, the remaining lies would still have made an impact. And the truth is, heterosexual life isn't always easier.

You may be thinking, well, okay, Sally, so you grew up with lies about yourself that you bought into and that helped shape who you are today. Lots of kids grow up with the same lies and they don't experience same-sex attraction. There has to be more to it than that.

I agree. Sexuality is complex and we haven't fully explored all the possible variables that enter into this equation. Biology sets a foundation, but the impact of what we experience throughout life continues to shape and reshape us. The dynamic interplay between chemistry, neurology, and our perception of life experiences over the course of a lifetime remains to be investigated. Mix in individual temperaments, largely a biological construct, and you quickly realize there are no cut-and-dried explanations as to how sexuality takes shape in us. All we really know, is that we have much to learn. And at the very least, our lack of understanding should move us to greater compassion. That's what makes this issue so difficult and complex. We've made a big mistake in trying, albeit with the best of intentions, to formulate cookie-cutter answers to the question of where homosexuality originates. There are no one-size-fits-all answers.

I believe God made each one of us so unique that the attempt to discover why we humans think and feel and behave the ways we do is endlessly fascinating. It's also exhausting at times, but fascinating nonetheless!

When I first began this journey twenty years ago, I wanted a "quick fix." I was ashamed of my feelings, and I wanted somebody to tell me what I needed to do to make them go away. I've learned it's not that simple. Replacing lies I've learned over a lifetime is as difficult for me as it is for anyone attempting to change a belief, a habit that they have come to accept as truth and reality. It's a long and arduous process, requiring conviction, diligence, patience, and emotional support. When something has been so conditioned over a lifetime, and at the very least compounded by biological influences, it's insensitive to think that someone could "just stop doing that."

We've all bought into lies about ourselves that direct the course of our lives in ways that God never intended for us. Depending on a host of factors that we experience throughout our lives, we will end up in different places, struggling with different temptations; but the base lies have all been the same. However, I believe wholeheartedly that replacing those lies with God's truth is in my best interest, and is ultimately what will allow me to fully experience all that God wants to bless me with in this life.

Our truest picture of self needs to come from God—a God who loved us enough to come down to live among us, to live sacrificially alongside us, ultimately giving himself to die in our place. "While we were still sinners, Christ died for us." Even in our most sinful state, we were worth the sacrifice, simply because we are God's children, his daughters and sons, heirs to the throne, a chosen nation, a royal priesthood. This is how Scripture describes us, giving us immeasurable worth to the God of the universe. If that's where my identity comes from, then the lies are, at the very least, uprooted.

Epilogue

I don't believe that being attracted to women was God's design for the expression of my sexuality. Nor do I believe that God intended for me to live out that expression in a sexual relationship with another woman. But there are times when I wish I didn't believe that. There are times when loneliness and the desire for companionship and intimacy rise to the forefront—when the desire for relationship that God placed within each of us longs to be filled in me. There have been times when I have given in to that desire. Yet in the midst of those times, my love for God, my conviction to follow him and live the life he calls me to remains unchanged. So I find myself living in the tension, the unresolved conflict of what it is that God calls me to in this life, of what it means to take up my cross daily and follow him, and the longings to be in an intimate relationship with one person for life.

The moments that have been the strongest, the longest, have always corresponded with a specific person—someone with whom I have first established a deep spiritual and emotional connection out of which a physical attraction has then evolved. It is in those moments that I have wished God would "change the rules."

I'm still filled with questions as to how to live the life of holiness that I believe God calls me to as a daughter of his who experiences same-sex attraction. Right in the middle of that tension, though, there is joy. There is peace. Because he is with me and nothing can ever separate me from his love.

Today I understand a lot more about how I got here than I did when I first began this journey of discovery nearly twenty years ago. I now understand how so many things influenced the development of my sexuality. I understand how relationships with each of my parents impacted me. I understand how watching my parents' relationship shaped my picture of relationships between men and women, and ultimately, my views about marriage. I understand how living in the midst of a family system that I perceived to devalue my gender influenced me, even though that wasn't at all what they meant to convey to me about femininity. I understand how friendships and media and experiences and conversations I overheard throughout a lifetime shaped my thinking about myself and my sexuality.

I also know the feelings that exist in me now were never my choice.

They just happened.

In this book I've shared some experiences that I believe contributed to the development of my picture of self, including my sexuality. This doesn't mean that this is true for all people who experience same-sex attraction. It may not be true for anyone but me. But it may be that someone else out there can relate, even if only in part, to my story. And if that helps anybody feel less alone, then it was all worth it.

A place to belong. Isn't that what we all want, really? Somewhere we feel loved and wanted. A place where we can be real. A place where we can say what's really going on inside and not be turned away or ostracized simply by others' silence. A place where we're included and accepted, no matter what.

That's what Jesus did for people while he was here on this earth. And he's still doing it today through communities of faith that believe in being safe places. CenterPeace is built on the concept of table fellowship, on the truth that Jesus invites each of us, no matter where we are in our thinking, to dine with him.

Center · Peace
a place to belong

CenterPeace provides safe places for men and women who experience same-sex attraction. Since 2006 CenterPeace has been helping churches and families all over the world learn a more Christ-like response to individuals experiencing same-sex attraction.

Founded by the author as a 501(c)(3) non-profit organization, CenterPeace offers seminars to help church leaders, educators, and families better understand same-sex attraction and open conversations about faith and homosexuality. Spiritual formation retreats are offered to provide community among fellow believers who experience same-sex attraction and are seeking deeper relationship with God.

Sally Gary serves as executive director of CenterPeace. She speaks to churches, schools, and university groups across the country. For more information visit our website at www.centerpeace.net or follow us on Facebook at facebook.com/centerpeaceinc and Twitter at centerpeaceinc. To schedule a CenterPeace seminar or speaking engagement with Sally, email her at centerpeaceinc@gmail.com.